PROCLAIMING
THE KINGDOM

A ROADMAP FOR BEARING
GOD'S MESSAGE
AMONG ALL PEOPLES

RYAN SHAW

FOREWORD BY MIKE ADEGBILE

IGNITE media

Proclaiming the Kingdom: A Roadmap For Bearing God's Message Among All Peoples
By Ryan Shaw

Published by IGNITE Media

GMMI
100 County Rd. 263
Armstrong, MO 65230
www.globalmmi.com

First print 2018, Copyright 2021 by IGNITE Media
All Rights Reserved

ISBN: 978-1-956435-07-8

All Scripture quotations are taken from the New King James Version. Copyright 1982, Thomas Nelson,Inc.

Cover Design – Bew Kanokkan Puranawit
Formatting Design - Acts Company, Chiang Mai, Thailand

More copies of this writing can be ordered from www.globalmmi.com or by contacting info@
www.globalmmi.com

Ryan Shaw can be personally contacted at rshaw@GlobalMMI.net.

In *Proclaiming the Kingdom*, Ryan Shaw skillfully explores the message of the Kingdom, making an effective case for the proclamation and demonstration of the Kingdom in fulfilling the Great Commission. While the Gospel of the Kingdom has been at the center of debate historically, Ryan's five-phase framework for bearing the message of the Kingdom is refreshingly rich with biblical insight and clarity. *Proclaiming the Kingdom*, therefore, is an important contribution to the Asian Mission and Evangelism movement and a timely exhortation for the Body of Christ worldwide. I commend this book wholeheartedly. Gloria Deo.

Mahesh De Mel - Director – Missions, National Christian Evangelical Alliance of Sri Lanka (NCEASL)

TO BE MORE INVOLVED, BE MORE INFORMED. It is highly improbable for God to lead one beyond the level of information and knowledge one has. In *"Proclaiming the Kingdom"*, Ryan provides some profound information as to how to be involved in God's unchanging and primary task for His Church - The Great Commission. Ryan should know, he is involved. Get informed, get involved, read this book!

Sam Kputu - International Director, CAPRO Missions

"Proclaiming the Kingdom is a breath of fresh air for cross-cultural mission. We talk much about strategy, culture and technique in mission yet often forget the message of the Gospel itself is what is powerful and transforms whole people groups. This book asks the question why the gospel is not having as much impact in our contemporary context as in the times of the early church. Ryan proposes an answer by relooking at the perspective of the Kingdom of God and providing a helpful fivefold phase by phase roadmap for believers to actively and accurately communicate the Gospel in its fullness among the lost."

Dr. Wati Longkumer – General Secretary, India Mission Association (IMA)

TABLE OF CONTENTS

FOREWORD

By Mike Adegbile

If you are a Mission practitioner or educator concerned about the fundamentals of the Gospel message we bear among unreached and unengaged peoples, and how the mass of lost and unsaved peoples of the earth can experience the Gospel in a culturally relevant way, Ryan Shaw's *Proclaiming the Kingdom, a Roadmap for bearing God's message among all peoples* has some good news for you.

Quite apart from a slanted gospel message that is lacking in the essential components of the biblical whole, the author argues that a comprehensive exposition of the Gospel message that is faithful to biblical revelation and communicated within relevant context, is required for the Gospel to have its intended impact on the hearers. That as people tasked with the responsibility to bear the Gospel to the whole earth, knowing the Gospel in its purest form and communicating it in culturally relevant ways, is crucial to experiencing a great global harvest.

In *Proclaiming the Kingdom*, you will discover the Gospel is about the Kingdom! Jesus' Gospel was the message of the Kingdom. Throughout His life and ministry, the Kingdom of God was Jesus' primary concern, inspiration, passion and purpose. In the same vein, the Kingdom was the thrust of Apostle Paul's message. Acts 19:8 reveals, *"And he (Paul) went into the synagogue and spoke boldly for three months, reasoning and persuading concerning the things of the kingdom of God."* Ryan argues that since the Kingdom was evidently the essence of Jesus' and Paul's message, it should also be our primary motivation and message among unreached and unengaged peoples.

The author did a masterly job to help readers have a proper understanding of the meaning, nature and message of the Kingdom of God as well as the now and the not yet of the Kingdom; that the kingdom of God has already broken into the present world in the person and work of Jesus Christ, though the definitive rule of God is still to come. That though the Kingdom of God belongs to the age to come, however through Jesus' first coming to inaugurate His Kingdom, this present evil age has been invaded by the power of that age, delivering mankind from its bondage, sin and death. *"Thy Kingdom Come"* is a prayer for the fullness of God's reign which is not yet experienced in the world. Ryan brilliantly submits that the Gospel isn't just for evangelistic purposes alone but the subsequent, comprehensive development of true disciples living their calling and purpose as citizens of the Kingdom of God. And that the Gospel of the Kingdom provides a roadmap for experiencing God's fullness as intended in the heart of God.

In *Proclaiming the Kingdom*, Ryan advocates that the responsibility for proclaiming a culturally relevant message of the Kingdom to the hearer's worldview rests with all believers irrespective of class, positions or race and this has to be carried out with the dynamic power of the Holy Spirit to produce faith in God that endures eternally. Sadly, so few unreached ethnic peoples come in contact with the living God in a culturally relevant way because so little of the Church's witness is done in the power of the Holy Spirit. Away from communicating the Kingdom from human ability and intellectual power, the author calls on the Church to seek the outpouring of the Holy Spirit as at Pentecost, if we hope to spiritually impact our dying world.

With scholarly breadth and biblical depth of insight, the author presents a refreshing and inspiring thrust of the core elements and motivation in the *Fulfilling Great Commission* and how the Church should close in on the remaining unreached ethnic peoples of the world, with a view to see a disciple-making movement among them in our generation. This he said is the body of Christ finish line – the primary purpose for which the Church exists in this age. The author concludes with Five Phases for proclaiming the Kingdom which you will find revealing and educative.

This is a book that Pastors, Mission Leaders, Mission Trainers, Missionaries and lay people who are passionate to see a culturally relevant communication of the Gospel of the Kingdom, in the power and strength of the Holy Spirit, so as to see the fulfilment of the Great Commission amongst all peoples, need to have and study. This book will set your hearts ablaze with a passion to see the fulfilment of the Great Commission and position you for maximum impact in the effective communication of the Gospel of the Kingdom. I wholeheartedly recommend it.

Mike Adegbile

Executive Secretary, Nigeria Evangelical Missions Association – NEMA

Mike also serves on the Global Leadership Teams of the Global Mobilization Network- GMN, Global Diaspora Network-GDN, Global Church Planting Network-GCPN, Africa M24:14 Steering Team and V5:9 in Sub-Sahara Africa.

1

WHAT IS THE GOSPEL?

Billions of people globally have never experienced the Gospel in a culturally relevant way that would allow them to adequately respond to it. Even for many of those who have heard, it was not communicated in an approach that led to a true grasp of its significance. It did not connect in any meaningful way, so it was dismissed as unimportant. This book seeks to address this problem as the body of Christ partners with Jesus in fulfilling His Great Commission among all peoples.

As I travel internationally, I often ask believers a crucial question: *"What is the Gospel?"* As those caring deeply about the Great Commission, it is necessary to ask what message we are bearing among unreached and unengaged peoples. Is our message consistent with the biblical, New Testament "Gospel," culturally relevant to the hearer – or something altogether foreign to Scripture and hearers alike?

"What is the Gospel?" A basic question, right? As followers of Christ, experiencing the new birth, we ought to have a solid grasp of the fundamentals of our message. Yet, I generally hear a hodge-podge of parts of the Gospel but rarely the biblical whole. The Gospel is commonly reduced in its scope, appearing vague. In addition, preaching *the Gospel* has come to include a wide variety of messages and good works. There are many important causes in the world, yet we must be careful not to lose our essential message.

A common thread usually heard as *the Gospel* is an emphasis on eternal salvation. However, many limit the message to eternal life alone. The Gospel is much more comprehensive and exhaustive, covering the fullness of what God intends for all humanity, both in this life and throughout eternity. We are often guilty of presenting a slanted Gospel, providing a few points of truth while neglecting entire core elements and processes of the whole. Salvation is obviously the introduction, yet Jesus calls His body to equip all peoples of the world with so much more.

Often in cross-cultural evangelism, we communicate generic sayings like *"Jesus loves you"* or *"Do you know Jesus?"* What if that community has only negative, wrong stereotypes about Jesus, supported by their religious worldview? Will they be able to rightly respond to His love? What if they have no knowledge of Jesus at all? His love would hold no value to them. What if they have no concept of sin?

Even more detrimental is communicating some version of, *"Come to Jesus, He will solve all your problems, making your life easy."* Is this really the Gospel according to Jesus? What happens when life does not become easy? People get disillusioned with God, thinking He somehow failed them. Many have fallen away because they were sold a portion of the message without the full scope, buying into fanciful ideas of following Jesus. Failing to provide needed context – and the whole message – negatively impacts our witness.

Our global society has become increasingly fragmented. Our lives are broken into many realms: public and private; political; religious; family; work; and play. Each realm contributes a slice of our existence yet fails to satisfy the wholeness we crave. The fragmentation produces a loss of the drama underlying all history. We participate in our little worlds, with tunnel vision, unaware of the global drama unfolding around us or our role in it.

This is not only true of unbelievers. Many disciples fail to grasp the core essence of history, the unfolding drama of God, possessing a theology that veers all over the map. They hear multitudes of sermons, participate in many Bible studies, while some have a devotional life. They experience personal salvation, are born again, knowing something of what God has done in their lives.[i] They have core beliefs surrounding worship, fellowshipping with other believers, health and prosperity, and the need of taking care of the poor.

However, they are missing the exhilaration of the bigger picture of a world full of diverse peoples, an earth caught in the evils of sin, a history from before Creation to eternity, of the reason for their existence in such a world. It is rare to find a believer seeing themselves as part of a movement far greater than their individual existence, the progressing of human history giving meaning to their lives.

Our lives and ministries take on a more significant meaning as part of the great mission of God, His history-unfolding purpose of restoring the Kingdom of God on the earth.[ii] Our lives become reoriented from simply doing acts of service or witnessing a bit to being consumed with partnering with the beautiful God working out His global purposes among all peoples toward a particular end.

Why Is the Gospel Not Having Expected Impact?

Often, we are surprised the message doesn't seem to be impacting people as we had hoped. We know it is powerful, transforming lives, wanting others to experience it. We read the book of Acts and observe the New Testament church, inspired by the impact of their message. We consider periods of Church and mission history where great moves of the Spirit took place among unreached peoples with staggering effect. Why are we not seeing the same impact in our day, in our part of the world?

We sincerely communicate a portion of the message, expecting great results. Yet, often little seems to happen. Why? Could a factor be our failure to proclaim and demonstrate the whole message? Sometimes, those coming to Jesus quickly fall away, returning to worldly ways. They responded well but don't seem to have the rootedness to go the distance. Why? Might our failure to take new believers beyond the elementary concepts of the message into spiritual maturity be a reason? The negative impact of these failures often breeds unbelief among believers. We know the Gospel is true yet are subtly unsure it can really transform whole segments of Islamic, Buddhist or Hindu populations.

The Gospel is the hope and power of God, His breakthrough message for all cultures and peoples, creating faith and strengthening the inner lives and societies of human beings. As such, it is the living message the Church is entrusted with proclaiming and demonstrating among all peoples globally. Yet it is common to minimize the message as we are not sure people will understand its intricacies and depths. We give them what we think they can intellectually understand. "Just give them the simple Gospel" is a phrase often heard. This usually means limiting the message to its introductory elements without providing needed context and background. It also leaves out the call to press on to maturity in Christ.

God has revealed His core message to humanity in a way that all can grasp, from the least educated to the most. We don't need to simplify it for the uneducated. The Gospel is primarily spiritual, not intellectual, so education capacity is a non-issue. We want to be faithful to the essential message, trusting the Spirit to teach and press it upon the heart and mind of the hearer, no matter their literacy and intellectual levels. Thus, it is crucial that those spreading the message understand what it really is, knowing the Gospel in its purest reality. Armed with a clearer picture of God's message, we can better apply it to our ministry efforts among specific peoples, seeing greater fruitfulness.

Why a Gospel *of the Kingdom*?

Jesus taught more on the subject of the Kingdom of God than any other topic (He used the phrase *Kingdom of God* over 100 times.) The Kingdom was ever on His mind. When Jesus commenced His public ministry in Galilee, *"He began to preach <u>and to say repent for the Kingdom of heaven is at hand"</u>* (Matthew 4:17). When He first commissioned the 12 and then the 70 disciples on their ministry journeys, He sent them with these words: _"Preach, saying the Kingdom of heaven is at hand"_ (Matthew 10:7). _"Say unto them the Kingdom of God has come near"_ (Luke 10:9).[iii]

Jesus' very Gospel was the message of the Kingdom. _"He went out preaching the gospel of the Kingdom"_ (Matthew 4:23). He focused on the Kingdom in His parables (Matthew 13) as well as in His major discourses - the Sermon on the Mount (Matthew 5-7) and Olivet Discourse (Matthew 24-25). Throughout His life and ministry, the Kingdom of God was Jesus' primary concern, inspiration and purpose.[iv] It was through the Kingdom that He received His all-sufficient power. If we follow Jesus' public ministry in light of what He said, we quickly conclude every word, journey, action of blessing or judgment, was motivated by the Kingdom of God. It was the master passion of Jesus' life.

Not only was the Kingdom Jesus' primary message, it was also the Apostle Paul's. Acts 19:8 reveals, _"And he (Paul) went into the synagogue and spoke boldly for three months, reasoning and persuading concerning the things of the kingdom of God."_ In Acts 20:25-27, Paul tells the Ephesian elders at Miletus, _"And indeed, now I know that you all, among whom I have gone preaching the kingdom of God, will see my face no more. Therefore I testify to you... for I have not shunned to declare to you the whole counsel of God."_ Paul's message was one chiefly oriented to the Kingdom of God. Since the Kingdom was evidently the essence of Jesus' and Paul's message, we must ask if His Kingdom is also our primary motivation and message among unreached and unengaged peoples.

What Is the Kingdom of God?

The Kingdom of God, in its simplest definition, is the rule, reign and authority of God in the world, the sphere in which His rule is exercised.[v] God's rule and reign is experienced by human beings and communities through entering the Kingdom of God today as well as in the future (Matthew 8:11, 25:34; 2 Peter 1:11). His reign creates both a future (Matthew 8:11; 1 Corinthians 15:50) and a present realm (Matthew 21:31) where believers experience the power and blessings of God. God has inaugurated His Kingdom (His manifested reign and will) in this age through the life and work of Jesus Christ in the flesh. This makes the Kingdom of God available now to all in the present (Matthew 12:28). Yet, that Kingdom will not be known in fullness until Jesus' second coming in power and glory (Matthew 13:41-43, 24:29-31). God is never fully working only for the present but ever has the future fullness in mind as well.

The Kingdom of God is the realization of God's perfect will, under His supreme authority and the enjoyment of accompanying blessings.[vi] That Kingdom is what God intended for all creation (living in submission to the authority of God) from the foundation of the world but was spoiled through Adam and Eve's choices. The Kingdom is now hidden to the eye, experienced by faith (yet dynamic with great available power), but upon Jesus' second coming will be established visibly in awe and power (Revelation 1:7; Matthew 24:30).

God has declared that He will ultimately triumph over all things, specifically the nations (people groups). Psalm 22:27-28 reveals, *"All the ends of the earth will remember and turn to the Lord, and all the families of the nations will bow before Him, for dominion belongs to the Lord and He rules over the nations."* The New Testament confirms the ultimate Kingship of God. Jesus is revealed as *"the ruler of kings on the earth"* (Revelation 1:5) who upon His return will be openly seen as the Lord God Almighty, the supreme King reigning in open display.

The Bible reveals two ages of redemption history (Matthew 12:32; Luke 20:34-35; Ephesians 1:21): *this age and the age to come.* The second coming of Jesus divides these two ages. The whole sweep of history is held in the hand of God, and the Bible looks toward the ultimate manifestation of the Kingdom of God in a new and different order of existence than known at present. The Kingdom belongs to the age to come, however through Jesus' first coming to inaugurate His Kingdom, this present evil age has been invaded by the power of that age. We can now experience a down payment of the age to come. We can be delivered from this age (Galatians 1:4), no longer conformed to it (Romans 12:2).

The present age is described in the Bible as under the dominion of the "god of this age" (2 Corinthians 4:4), yet we can already experience the powers of the age to come.[vii] Jesus has defeated the power of Satan through His death on the cross (Hebrews 2:14). The kingdom of Satan is still in effect yet has been, in a very real way, curtailed and inhibited through Jesus' work. The Kingdom of God has invaded the kingdom of Satan, delivering us from his power, bondage, sin and death.

Jesus' life and ministry demonstrated and proclaimed the authority and rule of God, His Kingdom. He explained it, revealed it, invited men and women toward it, while warning of the dangers of neglecting it. Even through His crucifixion, Jesus' passion for the rule, reign and ultimate authority of God was on display. His miracles and demonstrations of power revealed the Kingdom of God was real and available in the world. His supreme mission in the world is to restore the lost order and to establish the Kingdom of God, redeeming men and women under the rule, reign and authority of God.[viii]

Pushing Beyond the Boundaries

The biblical context of the expansion of the Gospel of the Kingdom is always beyond the current boundaries. The Church, born at Pentecost in Jerusalem, through the outpouring of the Holy Spirit, quickly spread among Jews in Jerusalem (Acts 3-8), to Jews in surrounding areas of Judea and Samaria of Galilee (Acts 8-11) and further still among Jews while beginning to be dispersed for the first time among Gentiles (non-Jews) (Acts 12-28).

The Gospel of the Kingdom provides a roadmap for experiencing God's fullness as intended in the heart of God. The *Gospel* isn't merely for evangelistic purposes alone but the subsequent, comprehensive development of true disciples living their calling and purpose as citizens of the Kingdom of God in the here and now. Problems have emerged because we have approached the Gospel primarily in terms of people coming to saving faith while neglecting the equally crucial aspect of leading them on to spiritual maturity in Christ's Kingdom.

The Witness of the Kingdom

The message of the Kingdom is often muddied and unclear. We are not called to communicate doctrine nor merely teach about "Christianity" as a religion.[ix] The Gospel of the Kingdom is the revelation of a Person to the world. A Person we were created to enjoy the heights, depths, widths and breadths of ultimate relationship with. The Holy Spirit uses those encountering Him in their own experience as His witnesses. Believers are an expression of experiential power more than intellectual instruction.[x] The Gospel is at times reduced to reciting facts about what God has done. Though facts are important, they are a biblical "witness" only when believers experience their truth, communicating them to others. The Holy Spirit demonstrates truths of the Gospel through believers' lives, proving them real. We proclaim the power of Christ to deliver, redeem, restore, persuading ethnic peoples to experience the fullness of God they were created for. The Holy Spirit takes the witness of Christ's power, impressing upon hearers' practical ways it applies in their situations, how its truth can bring experiential power and deliverance.

We have tended to limit the witness of the Gospel to the responsibility of pastors, leaders, evangelists and professional missionaries. However, the Bible maintains all believers – educated or not, illiterate or not – who have experienced the new birth are meant to proclaim the King and His Kingdom. The early Church, scattered from Jerusalem because of persecution (Acts 8:1), experienced great growth in the book of Acts, not due to apostolic leadership but because every believer took their responsibility to "gossip" the Gospel everywhere they went (Acts 8:4) – the marketplace, streets, neighbors, extended families, poor, professionals and more. The Gospel of the Kingdom runs swiftly through common believers, providing a simple, experiential witness of Jesus' power to deliver and restore.

Two Types of Witness

The New Testament includes at least two defining factors of a *witness*. The proclamation is culturally relevant to the hearer's worldview and is in demonstration of the Spirit and of power. It is this second factor we want to focus on here. In 2 Corinthians 2:4-5, Paul instructs, "*My speech and my preaching were not with persuasive words of human wisdom, but in demonstration of the Spirit and of power, that your faith should not be in the wisdom of men but in the power of God.*" Preaching here does not primarily refer to speaking to crowds of large numbers. It includes a common believer talking with two or three others in a village, university, online chat group, coffee shop or the like. Most believers will never speak to thousands but with individuals and groups of two, five, 10 or 20. Every believer is in view here.

Paul reveals two types of proclamation and two corresponding results in people's lives. The declaration is either in human wisdom (abilities, logic, etc.) or in demonstration of the Spirit and power. The corresponding result is either growing faith in people or in the power of God. These verses reveal one of the single greatest factors behind the current spiritual malaise in the body of Christ as well as the often small spiritual impact being made. We tend to communicate from *human ability and intellectual knowledge* rather than *in demonstration of the Spirit and power.* The principle is clear – *the spiritual life of the message bearer directly affects the faith of the hearers.* Only the Holy Spirit, working through a surrendered disciple, can impact another human spirit. Only communication in demonstration of the Spirit and power produces faith in God that endures.

When "witnessing" using human understanding, ability and logic, the faith of hearers is in human wisdom, consequently weak. When communicated in demonstration of the Spirit and power, the faith of hearers rests in the power of God, strong, stable and eternally enduring. Human wisdom, ability and knowledge do little to impact a human heart toward God – even when words are doctrinally correct.

Demonstration of Spirit and power refers to words, originating from the Holy Spirit, acting as a hammer, sword, or fire, cutting to the heart with conviction. Communicating God's Word using human ability and persuasion might produce thought-provoking ideas, but are unable to bring lasting spiritual transformation. How many consistently hear truth, yet are not cut to the heart, seeing themselves rightly from God's perspective? How many fill local ministries every week, knowing facts of the Bible, yet not living under the reign of the Kingdom of God in daily life? How many preachers are stirred with human emotion, producing little spiritual fruit that remains? How many believers put more faith in human wisdom of leaders than the power of God?

In Acts 2:37, on the day of Pentecost, Peter experienced preaching in the demonstration of the Spirit and power. Hearers _"...were cut to the heart and said to Peter and the apostles, brethren what shall we do?"_ Peter had just experienced the outpouring of the Holy Spirit. Pentecost was the establishing of the Church, and the Holy Spirit was the power of its new life. Peter witnessed of Christ with spiritual authority, power and fire, gripping the crowd, bringing great conviction. Because so little of the Church's "witnessing" is done in the power of the Holy Spirit, so few unreached ethnic peoples come in contact with the living God in a culturally relevant way.

Every plant grows out of the root it first sprang from. The outpouring of the Spirit at Pentecost is that root which the whole Church must return if we hope to spiritually impact a dying world. We long to see unreached ethnic peoples experience the power of God's Word as a hammer, sword, and fire, cut to the heart, brought into eternal fellowship with the Lamb as intended in the heart of God. Let's next consider the sum total of the global body of Christ's assignment here on the earth.

2
FULFILLING THE GREAT COMMISSION

Jesus announces in Matthew 24:14, *"And this Gospel of the Kingdom will be preached in all the world as a witness to all the nations, and then the end will come."* The whole of chapter 24 is Jesus' answer to the disciples' questions about the end of the age. Jesus reveals a generation of unprecedented difficulty and challenge for the body of Christ, yet simultaneously the release of great global spiritual victory, unlike any other timeframe, leading to the fulfillment of the Great Commission. In this verse Jesus unveils the particular message believers' bear among all ethnic peoples as a living witness – *the Gospel of the Kingdom.*

In Matthew 24:14, Jesus links the timing of His return with the Gospel of the Kingdom being experienced with unprecedented power among all peoples on earth. The whole New Testament bears witness to this same emphasis. The ultimate victory over all things is God's. The future Kingdom is His. Yet fulfilling the Great Commission is one condition Jesus has clearly provided us to His return in power and glory to the earth.

Matthew 24:14 reveals the body of Christ's role in the work. It has been said that, in any particular work, the Church cannot do God's part and God will not do the Church's part. There are things only God can do in His sovereignty but also responsibilities God commands His body to do. He will not do these for us. In Matthew 24:14, we see the natural outworking of spiritual transformation we have experienced in the Lord, a thorough commitment to ordering our lives around Jesus' vision of the fulfillment of the Great Commission.

The Church was established at Pentecost, through the coming of the Holy Spirit, as a missionary community existing for the purpose of enjoying God at the highest levels and proclaiming among all peoples the King and His Kingdom. Relationship with Jesus in the New Testament meant participation in His mission. He affirms this purpose by empowering His body to declare the Gospel, heal the sick and deliver the spiritually oppressed, marking disciples with His spiritual authority as part of the age of the Kingdom of God. This is the core purpose of the community of the Church birthed through Jesus' death, resurrection, ascension and the outpouring of the Spirit at Pentecost.[xi]

The fulfillment of Matthew 24:14 directly correlates with the vision the angel gave John of the throne of God in Revelation 7:9. *"After these things I looked, and behold a great multitude which no one could number, of all nations, tribes, peoples and tongues, standing before the throne and before the Lamb, clothed with white robes and palm branches in their hands..."*

Who is this *great multitude*? They are the fruit of the great move of the Holy Spirit at the end of the age, reaping the greatest global harvest in history. The vision John saw is the perfect culmination of God's promise to Abraham that *"in you all the families of the earth shall be blessed"* (Genesis 12:3). "All the families" refers to every ethnic people globally, rooted back to God's initial covenant with Abraham. What John sees is no small group. It is a great, uncountable multitude before the throne. The fact the Holy Spirit included the small phrase, *"which no one could number,"* gives insight into the significance of what is coming. Mass numbers, maybe more than 50% of the living population of every single ethnic people (all 16,000 globally), are before the throne. It is a common thought among believers that at the end of the age, there are only a small number of remnant believers. This is not what the Bible teaches. In truth, it will be the opposite as the Spirit moves with unprecedented power right before Jesus returns.

Disciple *All Peoples*

The *"Gospel of the Kingdom as a witness to all the nations"* (Matthew 24:14) refers to all *ethnic peoples* and is the same concept God promised to Abraham in the above Genesis 12:3 covenant. *Nations* in the original language is best translated *"ethnic peoples."* Jesus was not merely saying the Gospel would be proclaimed in every geopolitical nation but that it would take on a saturation effect within every individual ethnic people within every nation. The Greek phrase *panta ta ethne* is where we get our English phrase, "ethnic group." You and I are part of a specific ethnic group sharing language, culture, traditions and so on.

Statistics reveal more than 16,000 distinct ethnic peoples in the world. India alone is home to over 3,000 of these distinct groups. Of these 16,000 groups, more than 6,000 are designated as "unreached" people groups (other terms include "least reached," "marginalized" or "forgotten" peoples). An unreached people group is an ethnic people where the indigenous community of Bible-believing followers of Jesus lacks adequate numbers to evangelize and disciple the ethnic group at large. Believers are usually under two percent of the total population.[xii]

It's also helpful to consider "unengaged" people groups, of which there are believed to be around 440 remaining. There are no known believers or churches among these ethnic peoples, and the Bible isn't available in the local dialect. Most unreached and unengaged people groups live in the part of the world between the 10 degrees longitude and 40 degrees latitude lines on a globe. This giant rectangle "window" on the world covering most of North Africa, the Middle East, South Asia and Southeast Asia has come to be known as the "10/40 Window." The Gospel of the Kingdom is to penetrate all 16,000 global ethnic peoples, spreading like wildfire, with a large percentage coming to faith, gathering in multitudes of reproducing local churches. In doing so, the Kingdom of God takes root among each ethnic people, transforming its culture.

The Fulfillment of the Great Commission

Matthew 24:14 signals the *Fulfillment of the Great Commission,* directly connecting to Jesus' last command before ascending to the Father's right hand – His Great Commission (Matthew 28:18-20; Mark 16:15-18; Luke 24:46-49; John 20:21-23). The *Fulfillment of the Great Commission* is the body of Christ's finish line, the primary purpose for which the Church exists in this age, the focal point behind the unfolding of recorded history thus far. We must appreciate that final words carry considerable weight. This is why we value a person's last will and testament. Multitudes of Scriptures (Old Testament and New) reveal God's rescue plan of sending His Son to suffer as the penalty for humanity's sin, thereby restoring the failed relationship with God. Jesus completed His earthly ministry by giving His disciples a commission– our primary responsibility while He is gone. We are now closing in on all ethnic peoples having a living witness among them. This is the final, inspiring thrust of the Great Commission.

The fulfillment of the Great Commission in verse 14 must be understood in the context of Matthew 24 as a whole. Jesus describes the lead up to the "end of the age," when the greatest transition ever known will take place – from the "present age" to the "age to come" under the physical, visual leadership of Jesus on the earth. Our task takes place in the context of great pressure, persecution, challenge and difficulty. In His love, kindness and perfect leadership, Jesus forewarns us. The global Church engages in the Great Commission with eyes wide open, hearts ablaze with love, responding in faithfulness and obedience to the purpose of God in this age.

The Great Commission is not only for trained ministers and message bearers. Believers from every background are message bearers everywhere they go. The fulfillment of the Great Commission is the result of believers deliberately migrating with the Gospel. They purposefully relocate their families, businesses and professions to places with few believers. They live, work, raise families and unassumingly spread the love of Jesus, sparking church planting movements. This was how the early church in the book of Acts spread the Gospel and how we do so as well.

Core Elements

If Matthew 24:14 is truly a "finish line," what are the core elements related to fulfilling the Great Commission?

- Rapidly reproducing church planting movements (CPM's) among every people group producing a culturally relevant, vibrant, spiritually alive, multiplying community of believers (in a house, building, office or otherwise) in every neighborhood within walking distance of every person.

- The victorious completion of the translation of the Bible in the mother tongue of every person living on the planet – in audio and storying formats among oral tradition learners.

- Permeation of every people group in every place (every person hearing and seeing) with the Gospel of the Kingdom in a culturally relevant, age-appropriate way. This is accompanied by the demonstration of the Spirit and power (a result of God's people expressing the gifts of the Spirit like no time in human history) producing people movements to Christ of uncountable multitudes across every people group.

- "A great multitude" (several billion) of vibrant, wholehearted believers from every people group living as true, New Testament disciples reflecting authentic and apostolic faith, loving Jesus with all their hearts, and standing firm in the face of persecution, with joy and victory. A glorious bride made ready for her bridegroom.

- A large proportion of vibrant disciples voluntarily scattering themselves cross-culturally as message bearers (John the Baptist types preparing the way of the Lord) from every ethnic people group to other similar-culture people groups nearby with the Gospel of the Kingdom. They are salt and light and are not only traditional, professional message bearers but taking their jobs and families, deliberately reproducing church planting movements with the power of the Gospel.

- Breakthrough revival among Jews and a great proportion of living Jews coming to saving faith in Yeshua, living as wholehearted disciples (as a result of Jews seeing Arabs and other Gentile believers experiencing true faith, provoked to jealousy to embrace their Messiah).

A Global Harvest of 100 Million

A parallel passage to Matthew 24 is Haggai 2:6-9. The prophet looks forward to a day when the earth will experience a great shaking by God's own hand. This shaking includes all we have already seen in our Matthew 24 verses. The shaking creates an environment where the glory of God is seen and experienced at unprecedented levels, producing multitudes coming to the _Desire of All Nations_, worshipping and surrendering themselves to His leadership. The shaking (challenges, difficulties and trouble) actually produces the great harvest. This shaking is increasing throughout history. Yet, it is not all darkness. As the darkness and shaking increase, the glory of God is simultaneously being released, bringing about the release of light and power and the great harvest prior to Jesus' return. Many are praying for a global harvest of 100 million people from among unreached and unengaged ethnic groups, where there are presently less than 2% born-again disciples.

Crisis and Pressure

The Bible advocates pressure and shaking in individual lives, families, workplaces, etc., as a tool drawing them to Jesus. Crisis creates awareness of need in the human heart. The need was always there, but we generally do not pay attention when things are going well. When crisis happens and when our very lives may be at risk, we are apt to hear and respond to truth. This is how God will draw millions into the Kingdom in the coming years and decades. Yes, the challenges and distress on earth will be growing but, at the same time, a great throng from every individual ethnic people will be thrust into the Kingdom as the Gospel is announced in word, deed and spiritual power. Many will come to faith in the midst of crisis and even because of crisis. The pressure and crisis are part of God's design to produce the great harvest prophesied in both the Old and New Testaments.

Our Greatest Motivation

Matthew 24:14 provides the body of Christ with its greatest motivation. There is no stronger push for the fulfillment of the Great Commission than the fact that Jesus is waiting to return until the Church has finished her core purpose. Than the fact that this is what human history is moving toward. This verse is a rallying cry across the denominations, streams and networks in the body of Christ. Together, across the global Church, we give ourselves tirelessly to this glorious purpose, empowered by the Holy Spirit for this chief end. The Western and non-Western Church together push toward the finish line, knowing His return will closely follow. Jesus is waiting, yet the Church is content with business as usual – playing games with a few dedicated to this purpose but a majority content sitting on the sidelines. The process is clear – first, the fulfillment of the Great Commission through the chosen vehicle of His global Church and then the reign of Christ in His Kingdom. He will not fail to do His part, but He will not do our part for us.

3

A FIVE-PHASE ROADMAP FOR PROCLAIMING THE KINGDOM

Scripture provides a *Five-Phase* roadmap for proclaiming the Gospel of the Kingdom[xiii]. A "gospel" is an official announcement of something. In the ancient world, a "gospel" was an official declaration brought to a people from a king or ruler. It was given careful respect and attention. The body of Christ is proclaiming the Gospel of the King and His Kingdom to the world, its possibilities in the daily experience of every culture, sub-culture and people globally.

This *Five-Phase* roadmap is a useful grid, helping faithfully proclaim Kingdom authority among all peoples. It can be used in local churches, campus ministry fellowships, small (cell) groups, discovery Bible studies, discipleship schools, home groups, accountability groups, online groups and one on one. Because of the importance of every phase to the overall message of the Kingdom, it is helpful to break down the entire message into pieces. Each of the *Five Phases* includes many sub-truths toward seeing contagious people movements among entire segments of society within Buddhist, Islamic, Hindu, and atheist peoples, experiencing the King and His Kingdom, thriving as the body of Christ.

The following *Five Phases* contribute to the complete message we bear of the Gospel of the Kingdom:

1)   Phase One - The Kingdom has come near through the life and ministry of Jesus Christ, the Son of God made King.

2)   Phase Two - Human beings enter that "brought-near" Kingdom by being born again from above.

3) Phase Three – Those entering the Kingdom receive all the benefits, blessings and privileges of their new inheritance.

4) Phase Four – Citizens of the Kingdom are responsible to live according to its ways, principles and operations, spreading it among all ethnic peoples throughout the world.

5) Phase Five – The "brought-near" Kingdom in this age will be fully established in the world by a glorious transition to the age to come through the physical and visible return of Christ.

Skipping one phase or over-emphasizing another in our ministry process culminates in deficient disciples. We reduce the message to the detriment of those we sincerely want to reach. Doing so communicates a message not making sense to people. We may conclude we have been a "witness" and they are rejecting the Gospel when, in fact, we've failed to announce the whole message, leaving people stunted. It is common to find disciples deficient in faith due to the failure of those bearing the message to communicate all *Five Phases* of the Gospel of the Kingdom.

This process takes time. The truths of the *Five Phases* cannot be shared and demonstrated in one sitting. The idea of "giving the Gospel" in a one-time sitting has been part of our problem. In our modern world, we want the quick, simplified version. Yet, this leaves people malnourished. The phases and truths are communicated over time in the context of trust relationships through believers living for many years among those they are reaching. Muslims, Hindus and Buddhists alike piece the whole message together over time, experiencing the supremacy of Jesus and the Kingdom of God. Together, these five over-arching phases and their many related sub-truths contribute to the full message the body of Christ proclaims and demonstrates among all ethnic peoples and cultures.

Two Primary Activities of Our Commission

The *Five Phases* of the Gospel of the Kingdom can be divided into two portions focusing on two separate, yet related, activities of our global commission. In the most well-known commission passage, Matthew 28:18-20, Jesus provides a step by step blueprint: *"And Jesus came and spoke to them, saying, "All authority has been given to Me in heaven and on earth. <u>Go therefore and make disciples of all the nations</u>, baptizing them in the name of the Father and of the Son and of the Holy Spirit, <u>teaching them to observe all things that I have commanded you</u>; and lo, I am with you always, even to the end of the age."*

Among all peoples on earth, Jesus instructs two primary activities – *discipling and teaching.*[xiv] In verse 19, He commands the first activity, *"make disciples of all the nations."* The original language translates this more accurately as, *"disciple all ethnic groups."* From the former, we approach people in an individualistic way. We make "individual disciples" – one by one. Yet, the actual words of the first activity are best understood as *"disciple every ethnic people"* as a whole.

How do we do this? By living, teaching and providing examples of the Kingdom of God in their midst, looking for segments of the society responsive to the Gospel. We reveal the *Five Phases* of the Gospel of the Kingdom, with predominant focus on *Phases One and Two. Phase One* provides the background rationale of the work of the great King in creation, the fall of humanity into sin, and the vision and zeal of the King restoring His lost Kingdom, opening the way for all humanity to experience His Kingdom in their midst. *Phase Two* details the particular way human beings enter the door of that Kingdom through experiencing the new birth.

It is necessary to understand "discipling" as taking place both before and after people experience the new birth. We generally understand "discipleship" in Church terminology as what we do with those becoming believers. Yet Jesus Himself divided *"disciple all ethnic groups"* with the second activity of *"teaching them to observe all things I have commanded you."* He Himself gave us these two different activities, separated by the new birth. What modern church terminology usually means by *"discipling,"* Jesus called *"teaching."* Once believers are brought into union life with Jesus, crucial teaching and instruction takes place, guiding them along the journey of spiritual maturity. This is where the life of the Kingdom is intensively taught and experienced as the highest standard.

Thus, *Phase One* and *Phase Two* of the Gospel of the Kingdom emphasize the necessary introductory elements of the Kingdom of God, while *Phases Three, Four and Five* emphasize ongoing spiritual maturity that Jesus intends for every believer experiencing Kingdom life.

A Practical Plan for Engaging Peoples

Message bearers are committed to proclaiming and demonstrating the Gospel of the Kingdom among unreached and unengaged ethnic peoples globally. This might be in our home city, nation or a near or distant country. We rely on the Holy Spirit to lead. We focus on a particular sub-culture of that people. Ethnic peoples are obviously diverse. We identify a sub-culture sharing common age, values, interests, experiences and traditions. A skater community in Yangon, Myanmar; a community of prostitutes in Kolkata, India; a particular caste of an ethnic people in Colombo, Sri Lanka; an academic department at a university in Bangkok, Thailand; a Somali community in Toronto, Canada; a neighborhood of street kids in Karachi, Pakistan; internet technology workers in Delhi, India; a high-rise apartment block in Istanbul, Turkey; a Muslim village in Algeria; banking professionals in Shanghai, China; media workers in the United Arab Emirates or many other potential examples. The Gospel of the Kingdom has the best chance of *"running swiftly and being glorified"* (2 Thessalonians 3:1) along focused, relational, sub-cultural lines such as these.

We then look for those who appear open to spiritual things in these communities. We are purposeful about making relationships. We do this in a host of creative, focused ways, looking for felt needs through which we can help the community and subsequently build trust relationships. Consider ways to use online groups and platforms to connect with people. Ask the Holy Spirit how He would lead you to find those receptive to the Gospel among the sub-culture He has placed you. Most of the world's cultures are highly hospitable. Use this cultural attribute as an opportunity to connect with people in your targeted sub-culture.

Once you are getting to know particular people then deliberately engage receptive peoples in the above sub-culture (group) communities. Ask them if they have ever studied the Bible before. Most, when honest, have never done so. Then offer to meet with them to study the Bible one on one or in small groups (3-5 people). Perhaps meet weekly or twice a week to consider the sub-truths and the Bible passages referred in the roadmap together. This may be done in their home, your home, a coffee shop, their workplace or online through social media groups and platforms. Take advantage of the global online communication advances for the sake of the Gospel. A helpful method is to work through each of the sub-truths with others one by one. Each sub-truth includes at least one Bible verse or passage with its heading. Several other verses may be referred to in the description. Read the verses together and then consider the description, discussing questions, ideas, thoughts that come up. Use the verses and descriptions as a springboard for further considerations.

Helping unbelievers grasp the sub-truths of *Phases One and Two* requires meeting together, often for long hours, discussing, listening, building trust and understanding, over a period of time. Sometimes the process of their spiritually understanding is faster and sometimes takes longer than expected. All the while we are praying for the Holy Spirit to press Truth on their hearts, bringing the breakthrough of the Gospel, setting people free, growing them in spiritual maturity.

A Culturally Relevant Message

Next, we prayerfully take the *Five Phases* and their sub-truths, doing the hard work of prayerfully considering relevant ways to communicate within the worldview of the ethnic people, particularly the sub-culture.[xv] A common mistake is neglecting the worldview, or life perspective, of the people being reached. Worldview, in its most basic definition, is a particular philosophy of life or conception of the world. A people's worldview is the way they see and understand the world, especially regarding politics, philosophy and religion.[xvi] Worldview is affected by many factors: by a people's inherited characteristics, background experiences, life situations, values, attitudes, and habits they have developed.

In proclaiming the message, it is tempting to focus on pet doctrines and cultural expressions and forms of "Christianity" from our home context.[xvii] Every believer, local church, denomination and mission organization has culturally held expressions and forms of Christianity. They also have particular doctrines they prize the most. We naturally gravitate primarily to these when communicating the Gospel. Instead, these are laid down, replaced by a culturally relevant witness of Jesus' message of the Kingdom. We get into the shoes of the hearers, identifying with their worldviews, bridging the message to their reality.

We have generally expected ethnic peoples to understand the message from our particular cultural worldview instead of making it understood from their perspective. We are not true witnesses if failing to communicate in a way the hearer grasps as important and relevant. This does not mean watering down the Gospel. It refers to understanding how people see the world and finding bridges to the Gospel within their existing perspectives. God has put bridges to the Gospel within every ethnic people and sub-culture. We cooperate with Him by getting into the sub-culture's world, philosophy of life, and community. We adapt ourselves, verbalizing the Kingdom message so that it comes as "good news" to all (1 Corinthians

9:22). This is best accomplished through clothing the message in the cultural forms most meaningful and appropriate to the hearer. Muslims are approached differently than Buddhists, while Hindus have a different mindset than atheists. Each worldview is grasped with strategies from the Holy Spirit of how to bridge the Gospel.

There is always a tendency to add extras to the Gospel. Every person is born and raised in a certain culture. This includes how we dress, eat, relate to others, understand time, experience church and much more. We see our own lifestyle and expression of "church" and "Christianity" as normal and all others who are different as abnormal, inferior and strange. Whenever believers from one culture take the Gospel to another the natural question arises. Should others act like us in how they express their faith or be given freedom to work out issues of life and devotion to Jesus consistent with the Gospel and their own cultures.

We do ourselves a great service in cross-cultural ministry by identifying and removing cultural forms of the Gospel belonging to our identity that make no sense to another.[xviii] The message is reduced to truth itself, free from cultural hindrances often unknowingly added. This is difficult as human beings tend to be unaware of how worldview impacts our beliefs. It requires diligence to observe our own culture, identifying the many ways we innately add cultural elements to the message. Every culture has positive elements while also having attitudes and practices clearly against God's will. The Gospel penetrates a culture and is expressed through it while also transforming many aspects of the culture and lifestyle in opposition to the ways of God.[xix]

The New Testament is full of examples of how Paul and the early Church engaged cultures of their day with the Gospel. One example is Acts 17 when Paul is in Athens. After preaching to Jews in synagogues, bridging the Gospel to their fathers Abraham, Isaac and Jacob, Paul proceeds to relate with Stoic and Epicurean philosophers in a thoroughly different way. He uses the bridge of their "unknown god" to communicate the message in a way they could understand. He then expounds the Gospel from vs. 23-31 without ever referring to Abraham, Isaac and Jacob. The Jewish patriarchs were a Jewish cultural priority but not an Athenian one. Talking about them with Jews made perfect sense as doing so appealed to their sense of destiny in God. Yet, with the philosophers, Jewish patriarchs were not relevant, making no sense to their situation. Discussing them with the philosophers would have turned them off to the message.

Paul and the apostles never required new believers to stop being who they were culturally. It is an impossible expectation that sounds a bit silly. Yet, it constantly happens in cross-cultural ministry and is a significant obstacle to Muslims, Buddhists and Hindus coming to faith in Jesus. They wrongly believe (due to unfortunate words and examples of believers) becoming a follower of Jesus means giving up their culture. This is too much to ask of anyone and not Jesus' heart in the least. This happens partially because, in highly religious societies, these two areas (religious worldview and culture) overlap significantly. Muslims coming to Jesus possess cultural backgrounds that do not cease. Instead it is God's will the Gospel take deep root within every culture, redeeming and transforming it, removing the sinful elements. Jesus created and loves every culture, wanting to see the Gospel fully realized in and through every cultural expression, seeing that culture become all it was originally meant for in the heart of God. We must understand the difference between culture and religion in our outreach, encouraging the expression of the Gospel and faith in Jesus in all cultural forms.

Becoming Jesus' follower does not mean losing one's cultural identity or connection with the local community. It is through these very community connections that the Spirit wills the Gospel to flow most freely and effortlessly. Paul led the Gentiles of his day coming to faith in Jesus to conform to obedience to Jesus yet continue being who they were culturally. There were elements of the culture that went against obeying Jesus, and these the new believers were required to forsake. Paul planted reproducing churches that met people where they were culturally, never insisting they become something or someone else culturally. The churches thrived in the midst of ungodly situations, impacting multitudes from the same worldview, because new believers stayed engaged with the culture, transforming it, not separating themselves from it.

It is also common in cross-cultural evangelism to merely argue points of truth.[xx] This strategy rarely produces fruit. Instead, we point ethnic peoples to seek God regarding each point of truth in the Gospel of the Kingdom. We don't simply provide all the answers. We relate points of truth while guiding unbelievers to seek and find in God answers to their core issues. We teach them to pray themselves as the Holy Spirit can then drive home His truth among every culture of humanity.

4

PHASE ONE

The Kingdom Has Come Near

A big question the Gospel of the Kingdom answers is, *"How did we get here and where are we going?"* Every human being, no matter what cultural or religious background they come from, needs answers to these fundamental questions. The human heart knows it has purpose and is moving toward something significant. Apart from restoration in relationship with God through Jesus Christ, these purposes are muddied, producing confusion and frustration instead of intended peace, confidence and exhilaration. Jesus wants human beings knowing who they are, how they fit into the unfolding drama of history, and where things are going in the future. The Gospel of the Kingdom provides human beings every answer to these fundamental questions.

Phase One of the Gospel of the Kingdom – The Kingdom of God Has Come Near Through the Life and Ministry of Jesus Christ, the Son of God Made King.

Faithfully proclaiming the Gospel among all peoples, it is necessary to provide relevant background information. In *Phase One*, we reveal what God is truly like and why Jesus' life, ministry, death and resurrection is the strategy of God, restoring and healing the world. It is necessary to reveal the uniqueness of Jesus, as no world religion compares to who He is and what He has freely provided in Himself. All seek after God's satisfaction without finding it. They were created to experience true freedom in dynamic relationship with Jesus alone.

We go back to the beginning, revealing how everything began, what was in the heart of God, how things went astray, and the universal plan of God to restore the world and its peoples' waywardness. All major religions possess stories of how things began. Creating bridges to their stories, bringing in distinctive truth related to Jesus, is the necessary foundation of the Gospel of the Kingdom. Let's consider a number of key sub-truths of this initial phase of the Gospel.

A. Creator God Is Rightful King (Genesis 1-2)

The Gospel of the Kingdom begins with Creation. The true, Creator God is rightful King over all, deserving honor, glory and obedience from all humanity *by the sheer fact of being Creator*. In Psalm 47:2, the writer exuberantly declares, *"He is a great King over all the earth"*, and in Psalm 24:1, David reveals, *"The earth is the Lord's, and all its fullness, the world and those who dwell therein."* Creation was the first step of the eternal God's self-disclosure to all peoples through which He reveals His existence before anything else was.[xxi] He is maker of all that is visible and invisible (Genesis 1:1; Colossians 1:16), and His authority alone, motivated by love, brought all things into being (Genesis 1:3 forward).[xxii] Human beings' conception of God is incomplete without the marvels of His creative acts and loving care demonstrated for all He has made.

As God created, He repeatedly remarked, *"It was good"* (Genesis 1:4, 10, 12, 18, 21, 25). The God who "created" all that was good at the beginning continues to "create" in a powerful way among all peoples. His creative activities are seen all about us, benefitting the human race, revealing Himself as Supreme and the only true God, reiterating, *"There is no god apart from me, a righteous God and a savior, there is none but Me"* (Isaiah 45:21).

God's rule over individuals, families, cities, peoples, and nations is always righteous and just. All He does reflects His character. His power and goodness, holiness and justice, patience and mercy are always motivated by His concern for the interests of His Creation and Kingdom. The vast perfections, intricacies and complexities of Creation reveal a God full of wisdom, creativity, beauty and might. He Himself holds the whole Creation together as its very Source, providing sustenance for all (Colossian 1:17; Hebrews 1:3). Creation is of Him and for His praise and glory (Colossians 1:16), revealing the splendor and glory of the one true King (Psalm 8; Psalm 19).

It is far-fetched to affirm no God exists who spoke and set everything in motion. That somehow the order, complexity and detail of Creation simply happened of its own accord is sheer foolishness. When one recognizes these things, there is only one response. *"For since the creation of the world His invisible attributes are clearly seen, being understood by the things that are made"* (Romans 1:20).

B. What Is the Kingdom of God?

Through Creation, the King established a Kingdom for the blessing, enjoyment and highest experience of life by human beings for all eternity. The Garden of Eden (Genesis 2:8-9) was the perfect manifestation of the Kingdom of God in complete operation on the earth. The Garden, its perfections (free of all corruption, decay, sinful tendencies, curses) and unhindered face-to-face relationship of human beings with God, was God's intent for human beings for all time.

The Bible reveals two ages of redemption history; this present age and the age to come (Matthew 12:32; Luke 20:35; 1 Corinthians 2:6; Ephesians 1:21). The second coming of Jesus divides these ages (Matthew 24:30). The Kingdom of God belongs primarily to the age to come, yet through Jesus' first coming to inaugurate His Kingdom, this present age has been invaded by the power of that age (Hebrews 6:5). Men and women can experience the blessings of the age to come now (Ephesians 1:14). The kingdom of Satan is working (Ephesians 6:12) in this present age, however the Kingdom of God has invaded the kingdom of Satan through Jesus' first coming, enabling human beings to be delivered from his evil power, bondage, sin and death (Colossians 2:15). We can be set free from the influences of this age (Galatians 1:4), no longer being conformed to it (Romans 12:2).

The Kingdom of God is the redemptive rule of God in Christ, destroying His enemies and bringing the blessing of His reign to His people. *The goal of all history is the in-breaking and establishing of the complete manifestation of the Kingdom of God on earth in the age to come* (Romans 8:22). Yet, human beings are privileged to experience a measure of the future Kingdom's blessings in the midst of this present age.

C. The Creation of Human Beings (Genesis 1:26-27)

God created all human beings in His image to enjoy unhindered fellowship and relationship in His Kingdom for all eternity. The human race was created in love to enjoy God's presence (Psalm 16:11), under His kingly rule, for His glory. When God looks at human beings, He sees His own nature. No other creature in nature is distinguished this way. Human beings are the crown jewel of Creation, meant to live face to face, unhindered, with our great King, Most High God and Creator of all.

Through God's creation of Adam and Eve, He revealed a dynamic relationship between men and women that is a reflection of His divine image.[xxiii] God's design is for human beings to live in social interaction with one another in obedience to the will of God. The essence of a person's humanity is responsibility to others and the longing to seek relationship with God. Creation is significant because it reveals all peoples possess the right to know the God who set all things in motion and whose image they bear.

Human beings are innately aware of a divine being we are created to experience fellowship with. This is the reason behind so many religious expressions globally. Deep desire persists in human beings as religion does not meet the need. Every human being is meant to experience the perfections, joys and glories of God's Kingdom in full, relating with the one, true King who brought them into being at the highest levels of love. He created human beings to love Him freely, possessing a sense of dignity and choice. Yet, He pursues us, zealous to win our hearts, orchestrating circumstances in life to reveal His vast love, tirelessly seeking to draw us to ultimately choose Him.

All peoples globally have their origin in Adam and Eve at Creation. Together, we make up one large family. It is a betrayal of our common heritage to believe we are superior to others, looking down on them as lower, even worthless. The unity of the human race is an important truth. We do not exploit, demean or in any way subjugate others. Through the centuries, peoples began to perceive themselves as superior to others, developing nationalistic, racial loyalties among distinct peoples, producing destruction in the world.

D. Ruling the Earth (Psalm 8:6-8)

God purposed human beings to rule over the earth (Genesis 1:26, 28). In Psalm 8:6-8 David iterates with the same truth, _"You [God] put everything under his [human beings'] feet, all flocks, herds and the beasts of the field, the birds of the air, and the fish of the sea, all that swim the paths of the seas."_ In the Garden of Eden, God gave Adam and Eve activities to engage in, reflecting His desire that human beings partner with Him in overseeing the created order. Adam and Eve were to be married and procreate, work (subdue, till, guard), name the creatures, and rule over Creation. This obligation continues through their descendants (the global population) as God calls all those bearing His image (all human beings) to the role of co-regents with Him over the world.[xxiv]

This calling was muddied through the fall of Adam and Eve into sin. The human race was meant to extend its rule over the earth under God's guidance and for His explicit glory. Human beings possess a calling to rule over the earth today through partnering with God in Christ, bringing it back into subjection to His Kingdom.

E. Creation Reveals the Glory of God (Psalm 19)

King David exhorted human beings to look up, seeing God's beauty in His heavenly art gallery (Psalm 19:1). By looking to the sky, we catch glimpses of our beautiful God. *"The heavens declare the glory of God; and the firmament shows His handiwork"* (Psalm 19:1). We consider something beautiful when we feel attraction, admiration, delight, or a sense of marvel, awe or wonder. For example, seeing beauty in the stars attracts us to God. Job spoke of the Holy Spirit as the "Divine Artist," adorning the heavens: *"By His Spirit He adorned the heavens...These are the mere edges of His ways, and how small a whisper we hear of Him! But the thunder of His power who can understand?"* (Job 26:13-14).

All the beauty in the world is a token of ultimate beauty – God. The sky, sea, and mountains point to beauty in the future completely restored Kingdom of God in the age to come. They are a shadow of the perfect beauty openly displayed when Jesus returns. The universe is God's art gallery, displaying many colors, great energy, enormous sizes, and unfathomable speeds and distances in a number of stars that are incalculable. These facets display the beauty of God's creativity, communicating important truths about His personality. When we see Jesus' beauty revealed in Creation, it causes us to desire to know, please, and give our all to Him.[xxv]

F. Creator God Is Three in One (Colossians 1:16-18)

What is Creator God like? What are His characteristics? The eternal, Creator God, Most High over all, is One. There is none other deserving worship. All other gods and spirits are man-made creations of our own imaginations, infused with demonic power. He shares His glory with none. He is the living God, and worship of another is idolatry, rebellion against the Most High God.

Though Creator God is One, He is made up of three distinct Persons (All fully divine) – the Father, Son (Jesus) and Holy Spirit. All three were involved in establishing the created order. All three are pre-existent (before anything else was) as God, uncreated, setting everything in motion. Paul details this in Colossians 1:16, *"For by Him (Jesus) all things were created that are in heaven and that are on earth. … All things were created through Him and for Him. And He is before all things and in Him all things consist."* John 1:3 says, *"All things were made through Him, and without Him nothing was made that was made."*

The Father possessed the plan of Creation down to every detail, the Son vocalized the command, speaking it forth in His authority, and the Holy Spirit, hovering over the earth as the *power of God* (Genesis 1:2), acted on the Son's command. The triune God, in harmony together from the foundations of the world, brought all things into existence while continuing to sustain, uphold, care for and source the created order.

G. Creator God Is Loving, Holy and Just (Psalm 118)

Creator God is full of love, mercy, forgiveness and grace, even when we make mistakes, recognizing and confessing, forsaking them. He is kind and tender, patient, not wanting any to experience life apart from knowing Him. It is love that motivated the Creation from the beginning and love that propels it onward toward His coming Kingdom. All His attributes are rooted in love. He is all wise in His setup and government of His Kingdom, knowing everything in every human being's experience. He is all powerful, His power being known and experienced over all the spirit world, as nothing is greater than He.

Yet God is equally holy and just. He is perfect, with no mistakes or blemishes whatsoever. His holiness is represented biblically as a "bright shining light." Light is brilliant, clear, pure, radiating everything around it. His light is so bright the angels cannot look upon Him face to face (Isaiah 6:2). They cover their faces. To rightly relate with God, human beings must have a vision of His absolute holiness, majesty, splendor, perfection. This vision reveals how far we are from the perfections of God and our desperate need for Him.

We recognize we are separated from God by our wrong choices and actions and this gap between us cannot be bridged by anything that we do. We need a savior.

Because of His absolute purity and perfection, all that is imperfect cannot stand in His presence. He must judge those who stubbornly rebel against His laws, upholding His integrity as God – not because He wants to but because imperfection cannot relate with perfection outside of blood sacrifice. Because of holiness and justice, wrath and judgment exist against all remaining in wickedness, choosing rebellion rather than aligning with His ways.

Judgment is God seeking to awaken human beings to their waywardness, motivating them back to align with His perfections. People's attention is most awakened through painful circumstances. It is through these that God seeks to get our attention, helping us realize something is wrong, bringing us back to Himself. A sudden and unexpected reckoning is coming for all human beings when we die. God is absolutely just in His wrath and judgment as the world has failed to walk in His ways. His love, mercy and eternal kindness for the repentant sinner motivate His justice as He wants to wake us up now while we have opportunity to turn back to Him.

H. Characterized by Joy (Psalm 16:11)

King David described God's heart as full of joy and pleasure. Jesus is full of joy. His primary posture of heart is gladness (Psalm 16:11). *"In Your presence is fullness of joy; at Your right hand are pleasures forevermore."* *"Honor and majesty are before Him; strength and gladness are in His place"* (1 Chronicles 16:27). *"You give them drink from the river of Your pleasures"* (Psalm 36:8). The saints will live in the fullness of joy in God's presence. *"...Who is able to...present you faultless before the presence of His glory with exceeding joy"* (Jude 1:24).

God is merciful and gracious because He is full of joy. God's presence is full of joy because His personality is full of joy. Gladness and joy are at the center of Jesus' personality. Jesus walked in the anointing of gladness more than any man in history (Hebrews 1:9; cf. Psalm 45:7). Many think of God as being either mad or sad when He relates to us. How does God feel most of the time? This question is one of the most important questions in our spiritual journey. How does He feel when He looks at us? Our view of God's emotions affects how we approach Him in our weakness. Whether we run to Him or run away from Him when we face difficulty largely depends on how we view Him in His emotions. This impacts the way we feel about ourselves. The revelation of God with a joyful heart awakens joy in us. Peter described Jesus as having a rejoicing heart with glad speech. Jesus' primary disposition is gladness, not anger or sadness, and His primary speech comes from His gladness. *"Therefore My [Jesus'] heart rejoiced, and My tongue was glad...You [the Father]...will make Me full of joy in Your presence"* (Acts 2:26-28).

God delights in and has joy in His relationship with His people (Psalm 18:19; Isaiah 65:18-19) *"But you shall be called Hephzibah...for the Lord delights in you...and as the bridegroom rejoices over the bride, so shall your God rejoice over you"* (Isaiah 62:4-5). God relates to us in such kindness because He delights in lovingkindness (Jeremiah 9:24). The Lord has a heart of rejoicing for His people (Jeremiah 32:41). *"For the Lord will again rejoice over you for good as He rejoiced over your fathers"* (Deuteronomy 30:9).[xxvi]

I. Characterized by Humility (John 13:1-10)

God is clothed with humility. The concept of a humble God is unique to the Christian faith. No world religion emphasizes a God of humility; rather, they emphasize deities of power. We have confidence to relate to God because of His humility. Jesus didn't put on humility to accomplish a task on earth (the redemption of humanity). Humility is part of His eternal nature. He has existed eternally in the form of God as Servant. Daniel 7 prophesied that the Son of Man would receive leadership over all the nations (7:13-14). Jesus connected

His title as the Son of Man to serving people with humility. *"The Son of Man did not come to be served, but to serve"* (Matthew 20:28).

A servant is the greatest of all (Matthew 23:11; 5:5). Jesus will forever be the greatest servant with the most humility. In John 13, God showed us who He is in His core identity when Jesus took off His robe, girded Himself with a towel, and knelt before sinful men to wash their dirty feet (John 13). The world religions seek "gods of power," but *Jesus revealed the "kneeling God."* We can only understand truth about God as we see Him "kneeling as a servant" before His weak people. *"He...began to wash the disciples' feet, and to wipe them with the towel"* (John 13:5).

If Jesus' core identity was in showing His power, His incarnation would have been a denial of His true self. He did not serve to prove something but to express truth about Himself. It is precisely because Jesus is God that He served and gave freely to ungrateful men (Luke 6:35). There was nothing un-Godlike about washing the disciples' feet. He was at home doing this. Jesus is not out to prove a point about how powerful He is but to win the world's hearts for love. In His first coming, He did not come as the God of outward glory (Rev. 4:3) but as a Man who expressed glory by the mystery of humility. The God of glory wants relationship with every human being. He can amaze us with a show of power but cannot have relationship with us, apart from humility. The fact that God loves us and zealously wants our love expresses His profound humility.

J. Creator God Is Father (Matthew 6:8-9)

Creator God, who is rightful King, is intimate and merciful, near to those coming to Him according to His ways. He is superior Father over all (Matthew 6:9), caring for every detail, seeing all we are going through and helping us through. He is not far off, distant, unknowable. In fact, He is the opposite, creating all human beings to know Him at the highest levels of fellowship, fully known by Him. He is "Abba," or "daddy" (Romans 8:15). We do not need to be formal with Him. He delights that we find Him to be an intimate "daddy." His love has no bounds. We internalize the goodness, kindness and mercy God as Father has for us. He is love, willing to go to the utmost lengths for our good. As we walk in His ways, He perfects all that concerns us (Psalm 138:8). God as Father reveals the affection He has for us and that we, as trusting children, have for Him. He has our best interests at heart. Even beyond what we think is best, the Father knows best.

Conversely, we are His children. Human beings, created in His own image, are the recipients of His greatest affections. Though human fathers have failed us, God as ultimate Father has not. Though peoples have not known Him, He has known them, their history, pains, afflictions, exploitations. He is the source of their life, their existence. It is from great love that He willed their life into being, opening the way of restored relationship both now and for eternity.

K. Creator of the Natural and Spirit Worlds (Colossians 1:16)

Colossians 1:16 reveals, "_All things were created_ that are in heaven and that are on earth" and goes on to specify, "_whether thrones or dominions or principalities or powers._" God created all that makes up the natural and the spiritual worlds, including angels of every ranking, Satan and every evil spirit. Satan is a created being with significant knowledge and understanding (Isaiah 14; Luke 10:18-19; Ezekiel 28 and others). Satan stood in God's presence from eternity past as a high-ranking angel yet rebelled in pride against God, with one-third of the angels in heaven following his rebellion. Satan and these rebellious angels were thrown out of heaven, resulting in their rage against God, His Kingdom and people. Satan showed up in the Garden of Eden in the form of a serpent, tempting Adam and Eve to follow this same rebellion against God. He sought to usurp God's authority and control over the world and to derail human beings' calling to participate with God in its government.

Satan is not the opposite of God – he is not an evil, yet equal, counterpart of God. As a created being, he is far from possessing the supremacy and superiority of God. God is all-knowing, present everywhere and all-powerful. Satan and his demonic hordes are none of these. He cannot be everywhere at once, cannot know our thoughts, and does not possess all power. God is absolutely supreme, though He has given Satan freedom.

L. The Ultimate Purpose of Creation (2 Corinthians 6:18)

God's ultimate purpose in Creation was to provide a family for Himself, a Bride for His Son as His eternal companion to reign with Him in His Kingdom (Ephesians 5:31-32; Revelation 19:7-9). This present age concludes with a bride made ready for her marriage to Jesus (Revelation 19:9). Human beings receiving the restored work of Jesus through His cross and resurrection are part of that bride. Jesus' bride is an uncountable number of those, throughout history, walking in fellowship with God (Revelation 7:9). Jesus, the Lamb of God, looks forward to the consummation of that relationship through the marriage supper of the Lamb (Revelation 19:9). Following that marriage supper, the bride will experience face-to-face relationship with the Son of God for all eternity. His bride is now, in and through recorded history, becoming ready for the coming marriage supper of the Lamb.

M. A Kingdom Lost (Genesis 3)

Following Creation, tragedy struck. The first human beings, Adam and Eve, lost fellowship with God and His accompanying Kingdom, tempted by the evil one, choosing their own way (Genesis 3:22-24). God, in wisdom and love, created human beings with freedom to make choices, possessing dignity, choosing Him or not. God will never violate the free will of a human being. Yet, He told Adam and Eve explicitly the result of violating His command not to eat the forbidden fruit: *"For when you eat of it you shall die "* (Genesis 2:17). There are consequences to failing to walk according to God's ways.

Through Adam and Eve's choice, they decided for themselves what was good or evil instead of listening to God. They took God from the center of their existence, making themselves the ultimate authority, using this world to further their desires. As the ancestors of all people, through their tragic choice, the floodgates of rebellion, self-centeredness and Satan's activity were thrown open among humanity. Because of this staggering event, Paul declares in Romans 3:23, *"All have sinned and fallen short of the glory of God."* All are separated, cut off, deemed enemies of the intended Kingdom of God in the King's heart. It had to be this way because of God's holiness and righteousness. The intended Kingdom for eternity was lost in the experience of human beings as self-centeredness flooded the human spirit. Human beings, from that moment, lived consumed by lust of the flesh, lust of the eyes, and pride of life (1 John 2:15). They experienced incessant fear, brokenness in relationships, addictions, abandonments, perversions, hatred, emotional depression and more. Darkness, in all its terrible forms, flooded the human experience, causing untold pain and anguish across the centuries.

Through this event, the deceiver (Satan) took a measure of power, creating chaos in every heart, relationship and community. Though God is King of the earth as supreme Creator (Psalm 24:1), Satan holds sway over hearts and minds of human beings as "god of this age." Paul details in 2 Corinthians 4:4, *"But even if our gospel is veiled, it is veiled to those who are perishing, whose minds the god of this age has blinded, who do not believe, lest the light of the gospel of the glory of Christ, who is the image of God, should shine on them."*

Paul clarifies again in Ephesians 2:2, *"And you He made alive, who were dead in trespasses and sins, in which you once walked according to the course of this world, according to the prince of the power of the air, the spirit who now works in the sons of disobedience."* Satan, influencing human beings separated from God due to sin, continues to hold men and women in bondage to false ideas of truth.

Human beings experienced the loss of the Kingdom profoundly, developing man-made systems attempting to relate to the divine (religions), trying to fill the desperate void within (Genesis 11). These systems of false belief spread all over the world, holding people in bondage and darkness instead of guiding them to the true light (Creator God) they seek.

N. The Problem of Sin (Romans 3:9-20)

The disease of sin, inherited by every human being through the choices of Adam and Eve, is the human problem needing an answer. The fact of humanity's sin and depravity is ignored by some, even rationalized as non-existent, yet is revealed in our sinful speech (3:13-14) and actions (3:15-16), proving all are sinful (3:17-18). Paul emphasizes the doctrine of depravity (3:19) to show all are guilty before God (3:20). Human beings are not sick in need of healing. We are dead in need of resurrecting.[xxvii] We are marked, every one, by death working internally as well as externally. Total redemption is the only answer to the human condition. We realize the full meaning of God's grace only when we understand our sinfulness deserves God's wrath.

Sin is the root poison in our hearts motivating actions, behaviors and words against the authority of God. The external acts are *sins,* but the issue within is *sin.* The disease of sin has to be dealt with and is why Jesus died on the cross. It was not merely to wash the subsequent wrong actions, behaviors, and choices made (sins) but to put to death the root itself (our inherited sinful nature). Whether lust, anger or pride, all these come from the root of sin in the human heart. Human beings cannot merely try harder not to sin. It is possible to curb outward manifestations of sin seen by society as inappropriate. Yet, the rage of that particular area of sin is still there on the inside. This is due to the poison of *sin* within.

Humanity innately knows something within is not right, that they are separated from the divine by a wall. This is one factor motivating the proliferation of religious expressions. We are trying to connect to the divine by earning merit, doing good deeds, saying the right chants, offering the right rituals, appeasing the spirits and more. The poison, however, cannot be overcome except by blood sacrifice. Humanity innately understands the necessity of blood sacrifice to make one clean. This is why animals are sacrificed to gods and spirits in nearly every religious expression. But what blood is truly sufficient to cleanse the world of the poison of sin? Only that of the Creator King Himself who became a perfect human being.

The darkness in the minds of all peoples can only be driven out by the light revealed by Creator God. The death grip of the "powers" can be broken by the One who through His own death and resurrection *"disarmed all principalities and powers, making a public spectacle of them"* (Colossians 2:15). The guilt of humanity can only be removed by the One who was made sin for all and who received within Himself the judgment all peoples deserved.

O. God's Plan to Restore the Lost Kingdom (Genesis 12)

Though a devastating loss, the all-knowing King was not taken back by this turn of events. Creator God, supreme and all-powerful, possessed a plan of love from eternity past. His plan would in time restore the lost Kingdom, returning humanity to its rightful place of experiencing unhindered fellowship with the King, walking in the blessings of His intended Kingdom. He would reverse the curse upon humanity through the loss of the Kingdom. His plan would include complete victory in human history, defeating all enemies, establishing Himself as "King of kings and Lord of lords (1 Timothy 6:15-16)." He would in time bring His people into an ultimate "golden age of salvation."

In Genesis 12, God sets in motion His plan, spanning the rest of the Bible and covering at least 6,000 years of human history. God promises Abraham in Genesis 12:1-3, *"Get out of your country, from* *your family, and from your father's house, to a land that I will show you. I will make you a great nation, I will bless you, and make your name great. And you shall be a blessing. I will bless those who bless you, and I will curse him who curses you, <u>and in you all the families of the earth shall be blessed.</u>"*

God's restoration plan began with choosing Abraham as the beginning point of both salvation history and the history of the people of Israel, God's vehicle toward restoration (Genesis 12). God made several eternal covenants, which cannot and have not been broken, with Abraham (Genesis 15:1-6; 17:1-6), his son Isaac (Genesis 26:3-5; 26:24), and grandson Jacob (Genesis 27:27-29; 28:3-4; 28:13-15). God's restoration plan continued through supernaturally bringing this people out of the bondage of Egypt (Exodus 7-14) into a promised land (Joshua 1:5-9), setting up a governmental *Kingdom* representing His relationship with His people.

God's purpose was always that Israel, in covenant relationship with Himself as King, would be a conduit of light and blessing of His eternal Kingdom among all ethnic peoples (Isaiah 42:6). Israel was not created as a focal point of His love to the neglect of the rest of the world's peoples. Instead, Israel was to be God's channel, releasing His Kingdom love and purpose to all. Yet, due to Israel's failure and inability to follow His ways, God could not use her as He had planned. Their failure set the stage for the coming One who through a completely obedient life, a faithful witness in His generation, and His atoning sacrifice through voluntary death would establish a new covenant that would embrace all nations (Jeremiah 31:31-34; Ezekiel 39; 24-28).

The hatred of much of the world toward Jews is due, in part, to Satan's deceptions to thwart the purposes of God's plan of restoration. He sows confusion, fueling misunderstanding and subsequent hatred from peoples around her, while influencing Jews themselves to buy into a false narrative of supremacy before God and His neglect of others.

Israel's failure to be what God intended did not stop the King. His restoration plan for the lost Kingdom would be established through two successive developments. The Old Testament prophets looked to the future (hundreds and thousands of years before these events), referring consistently to either one or both of these certain developments: (1) The Kingdom coming near in this age through the first coming of Jesus (the Son of God), redeeming all who believe, hidden to the five senses, experienced by faith. (2) The Kingdom's complete restoration in visible, physical power and glory in the age to come, ridding the earth of all evil and wickedness, through Jesus' second coming.

Through the first development, the King would open the door for multitudes from all ethnic peoples to choose, of their own accord, to experience the Kingdom of God through restored relationship with the King. Through the second development, the King would bring in open, visible display the power and glory of the manifested Kingdom of God to the earth.

P. God Becomes a Human Being (Matthew 1; Luke 2)

The Old Testament prophets correctly predicted the first development of Kingdom restoration. Multitudes of Old Testament prophecies, spoken hundreds of years before Jesus was born, provide evidence of the uniqueness of this great plan of God. God's unfolding of salvation history would take a major leap forward through the extraordinary life and ministry of Jesus.

The Kingdom has come near in this present age through the first coming of Jesus to redeem those who believe (Hebrews 1:2). His life and ministry is a demonstration of the nature and purpose of the Kingdom of God. Jesus says about Himself in Luke 19:10, *"For the Son of Man (Jesus the Christ) has come to seek and to save what was lost."* Before His birth to Mary, an angel declares of Jesus, *"He will save His people from their sins"* (Matthew 1:21). His first coming provided a channel for restored relationship with God, restoring lost humanity fallen into rebellion.

Revealing the lengths He would go in love for Creation, God did something unprecedented, never seen or considered in human history. Demonstrating His wisdom, vast superiority and extraordinary love for all peoples, God became a human being, Jesus the Christ, living a perfect life, revealing the life of the Kingdom and ushering in all its benefits, blessings and responsibilities.

The infinite, omnipotent, omniscient King did not come to earth on a glistening golden throne but through the agony and blood of human birth. As every human being comes into the world this way He identified with humanity through the same. God did not merely reach part way to us in a distant way but all the way down into the stinking mess of human misery and depravity, becoming one of us.

In this history-shaking event, both the Father and Son did something extraordinary, counter to the ways of this world. *"And the Word of God (Jesus the Son) became flesh and dwelt among us and we beheld His glory, the glory as of the one and only of the begotten of the Father, full of grace and truth"* (John 1:14). This was an extremely costly endeavor. Jesus left the glory of eternity with His Father, coming to this broken, cursed and rebellious world, identifying with sinful humanity to save them and repossess the fullness of His Kingdom for all time and eternity.

He voluntarily (motivated by extravagant love) emptied Himself of divine privileges (Philippians 2:5-8). He came, not as a wealthy King but a sacrificial Servant (Isaiah 53:11), a King humbling Himself, revealing the true measure of greatness in the Father's eyes – humility, meekness, lowliness. He revealed a different kind of Kingdom, an "upside-down Kingdom," where those following Him would live an opposite lifestyle of the accepted values, priorities, norms and relationships of culture, embracing His ways of lowliness.

Jesus declared of Himself, *"Take my yoke upon you and learn from Me, for I am lowly and gentle in heart,* and you will find rest for your souls" (Matthew 11:29). The world's ways drive human beings to pursue fame, fortune, honor and power. Jesus reflects the eternal God and what His Kingdom and people are meant to be - humble, embracing lowliness, meekness. His humility continues as He hides His full-fledged Kingdom in this age, known by faith not by sight. This gives all peoples the free will due them to choose Him as dignified human beings.

His coming near, becoming like us, was with purpose - to reveal what God is like, to bring the reality of the Kingdom of God, to open the way for all human beings to be reconciled with the supreme God, to take back all things lost, through the fall of Adam and Eve, for Himself. Jesus Christ, fully divine and fully human, became like every other human being in all ways- except our inheritance of sin. Jesus was conceived through God's supernatural intervention, born into poverty, showing He came for all, especially the poor. He grew in wisdom under the supervision of a human mother and father. God was preparing Him for His ministry and purpose of restoring the Kingdom of God through shedding His own blood, subsequently overcoming eternal death once and for all.

Jesus' three-year ministry was characterized by sacrificial servanthood, compassion, love, miracles, truth, authority and power. His first coming was the greatest sign of the Kingdom of God among humanity to that point while His second coming will be the culminating sign of His Kingdom among us. He perfectly fulfilled the well-defined Old Testament role of messengers sent by God - Prophet, Priest, King and Servant. In addition, He took on key mission roles - Evangelist, Apostle and Teacher.[xxvii] His supreme authority as rightful King was demonstrated by healing disease, raising people from the dead, delivering from spirit oppression, and embracing the most outcast and rejected of society. These acts were signs to all that the Kingdom of God had come near (Luke 10:9).

No human being ever walked the earth who matched Jesus. Everyone He met was profoundly touched and impacted. He served everyone equally, with no favorites, based on the heart hunger they possessed. The coming of the Kingdom through Jesus reveals God's attitude toward poverty and injustice. The King's values are clear as He is loving, caring, concerned for human beings, inviting all peoples to be restored to Himself, subsequently aligned with love, never oppressing, exploiting, using others for their own gain. The King values life and hates senseless killing and the low value of human life found around the world. Because human beings are made in the image of God, all have innate value before the King. Through His life and ministry, the possibilities of the Kingdom of God were revealed before all humanity's eyes.

Q. Jesus as God's Perfect Representation (Colossians 1:19)

Jesus, the Son of God, fully human and fully divine, is the perfect representation of Creator God among humanity (Hebrews 1:3). No impurity is in Him whatsoever, no blemish, no taint of sin, no failure. His ways, motives, intents and plans are perfect, rooted in perfect wisdom for His Kingdom and love for human beings. Jesus lived His human life to reveal to the world what God is really like. Paul taught, *"For it pleased the Father that in Him (Jesus, the Son) all the fullness should dwell"* (Colossians 1:19). Not only does the fullness of God reside in Jesus, but God purposed to restore the Kingdom to human beings through the sacrifice and doorway of Jesus Himself (Colossians 1:20).

Jesus is also the perfect representation of all humanity is He is not only fully God but simultaneously fully human. He is the only Person to ever be fully God and fully human. God the Father nor the Holy Spirit have this distinction. Neither do angels or human beings. He is the only One to ever bridge the gap of complete divinity and total humanity. As a result, He can represent humanity before God as

He took the separation between God and humanity upon Himself, tearing the veil and opening the door for all who believe in Him to be restored to God.

R. The King Crucified (Matthew 27; Mark 15; Luke 23; John 19)

Through His ministry, Jesus proclaimed the reign of God, training followers to continue and expand His messianic community after His ascension. His three years with His disciples were meant to reveal what true discipleship was all about while also clarifying what it was not. His three year ministry was a crash course for all to follow and learn from in every way. Yet His life was moving toward a deliberate climax. *"Behold, I cast out demons and perform cures today and tomorrow, and the third day I shall be perfected. Nevertheless I must journey today, tomorrow and the day following; for it cannot be that a prophet should perish outside of Jerusalem"* (Luke 13:32-33). The sacrificial Servant had to embrace the core event so the Kingdom of God might be brought fully near. *"The Son of Man must suffer many things...and be killed"* (Mark 8:31). This was necessary due to humanity's separation from its Creator. Jesus' suffering was the culmination of the plan of God to achieve His greatest victory – the salvation of all peoples who believe.

The narrative of Jesus' life speeds up as He nears Jerusalem. The disciples thought Jesus' laser focus toward Jerusalem signaled the time had finally come for Him to establish a physical Kingdom in power and glory. His "triumphal entry" (Matthew 21:6-11) represented this hope for His followers. Yet, as that week progressed and Jesus was betrayed by Judas (Matthew 26:14-16), forsaken by the disciples (Mark 14:50), tried and brutally crucified by the Jews and Romans (Mark 15:1-32), the disciples' disbelief, confusion and emotional grief came to a head. The situation was a total disaster. Their faith was stripped to its lowest point. One disciple laments, *"We had hoped that He was the one who was going to redeem Israel"* (Luke 24:21). At the time, there was no sense among Jesus' followers that He was reigning through His death, that this event was somehow achieving the open Kingdom of God for all humanity. To His followers, all was lost, yet to God the initial phases of victory had been accomplished. In time, the disciples would grasp that as the sacrificial Lamb (Isaiah 53), Jesus established His claim of universal authority and Kingship.

How did things shift so quickly during that week? Jesus' teachings were in stark contrast to the Jews'. Their leaders had become corrupt, mishandling the truths of God passed down from Abraham, Isaac and Jacob, using them for their own ends (Matthew 23). They focused on external formality while overlooking the state of the heart. Jesus' teaching corrected them, revealing right understanding of Old Testament Law (Matthew 5:21-48). For this, they hated Him. Jesus threatened the Jewish leaders' power over the people. Their rage grew to the point of having Jesus secretly arrested, tried and crucified as a common thief (Luke 22:1-2). Jewish leaders, God's chosen people to reveal His Kingdom to all peoples, solidified their failure in God's purposes through crucifying the very King they were waiting for. Yet God, rich in mercy, does not forget His eternal covenants with Israel. He will restore Israel in Christ, surrounding the still future events of His second coming.

The sacrificial death of a perfect human being, God the King Himself, was the cost of the first development of restoring the Kingdom of God. No other sacrifice could satisfy the wrath of God. Jesus willingly (motivated by extravagant love) took upon Himself the terrible weight of the wrath of God, reserved for human beings justly separated from God, restoring relationship for all who believe with the eternal Creator God. This act reveals unparalleled love. Though humanity deserved the wrath of God, Jesus willingly took that wrath on Himself. Those receiving His work as their own experience salvation; those not doing so remain in their sins, guilty before God.

In the big-picture sense, Jesus was not put to death by the Jews or Satan. He willingly submitted to the will of God, deliberately allowing

Himself to die on the cross. This was God's plan to reverse the curse of sin for those who would turn and believe. Do not forget Jesus is God, the Creator King, who at any moment in the crucifixion process could have stopped the ordeal. Instead, God in the flesh, in humility and poverty, took the penalty of human rebellion against God for all who believe. This seemingly devastating turn of events worked in God's favor as His ultimate purpose of restoring human beings to fellowship in His Kingdom was achieved.

S. Known from the Foundation of the World (Psalm 139:13-18)

What motivated this extraordinary act of sacrifice? Paul reveals in Romans 5:8, *"But God demonstrates His own love toward us, in that while we were still sinners, Christ died for us."* He saw every ethnic people, family and individual from the foundation of the world, knowing us then and willing us to be brought forth in our mother's womb. God chose us that we should know Jesus, being holy because of Christ and His work (Ephesians 1:4).

Every person, no matter the family or whether or not our parents even wanted us, was conceived according to the perfect will of God, desiring relationship with each one. Jesus saw us and willed us into existence. Psalm 139:13-15 assures us, *"For you formed my inward parts; you covered me in my mother's womb. I will praise you for I am fearfully and wonderfully made. ... My frame was not hidden from you; when I was made in secret...you saw my substance being yet unformed. And in your book they were all written, the days fashioned for me, when as yet there were none of them."*

T. The King Resurrected, Forever Alive (Matthew 28:1-10; Mark 16:1-13; Luke 24:1-43; John 20:1-18)

Though an extraordinary gesture, Jesus' ultimate sacrifice is meaningless without the King taking a further, equally extraordinary earthshaking step. If God becoming a human being was unprecedented, then God raising Jesus from the dead, overcoming the power of death, was even more extraordinary. It is blasphemy for many globally that God could die in the first place. Jesus' death reveals the extent God would go in restoring His Kingdom. It is His resurrection that solidifies the purpose of His death. Through the resurrection God was validating Jesus' Person and ministry. The resurrection is God's seal of approval on all Jesus had said and done.[xxix] He is the only human being to be raised from the dead, never to die again. Jesus was faithful to all of God's will in restoring His Kingdom. Jesus, the supreme King, is alive today and will never, ever experience death again. This same type of eternal resurrection is waiting for all who believe in Him and His Kingdom.

Jesus' resurrection is the central triumph of redemptive history. Paul declares of Jesus in Romans 1:4, *"And declared to be the Son of God with power according to the Spirit of holiness, by the resurrection from the dead."* The disciples, experiencing His death and resurrection firsthand, were slow to understand their significance. Over time, they would grasp what Jesus was accomplishing through these events. *"God was in Christ reconciling the world to Himself, not reckoning their trespasses to them"* (2 Corinthians 5:19), He was *"disarming the powers and principalities, making a public spectacle of them"* (Colossians 2:15), *"destroying the works of the devil"* (1 John 3:8), and *"overcoming the world"* (John 16:33).

Through the cross and resurrection, the God of inexhaustible love purchased back the lost Kingdom to Himself, making a way for human beings to experience the original purpose of all humanity for all time – *The Kingdom of God.* Jesus' work through the cross and resurrection is the greatest gift of mercy human history has ever seen. While all religions seek in vain to get to God, God has taken the initiative of coming to us, breaking down the wall of division by becoming a perfect human being. He died in our place on a vicious cross, overcoming death through physical resurrection for all who follow Him.

U. Events Following His Resurrection (Acts 1:1-3)

Following Jesus' death and resurrection came a period of 40 days when Jesus encouraged the faith of the disciples, teaching them crucial elements of the Kingdom of God (Acts 1:3), before visibly ascending to the right hand of God. During this period, He revealed three primary areas of truth.

First, He revealed Himself as the center of Old Testament revelation. Believers needed to understand the unity of the Old Testament and the new revelation in Jesus Himself (Luke 24:25-27). Jesus would have taught more deeply about His own Messiahship from the Old Testament. He would have revealed how Messiah was to be the "Suffering Servant" of Isaiah 52 and 53 and how this process was the only way He could fulfill His purpose and restore the Kingdom of God. He was helping them put the pieces together of how Messiah could have suffered and what the meaning and implications behind it all were. The Holy Spirit would be given to help _"guide them into all truth"_ (John 16:13) related to the correlation of the old and new. There were many matters Jesus still had to teach them (John 16:12), and the Spirit would take over this role in the coming days, months and years.

Second, Jesus gave the disciples the Great Commission, the mandate of the whole body of Christ between Jesus' first and second comings. The commission was entrusted to all who call on the name of the Lord. We proclaim the Kingdom among all peoples, discipling, baptizing and teaching them (Matthew 28:18-20), gathering disciples into living fellowships called churches, pursuing the planting of a church within walking distance of every human being on the planet.

Though He gave this official commission just prior to His ascension we know Jesus taught the disciples Old Testament passages like Genesis 12:3, 22:18 and 26:4, where blessing to all the world's peoples (not merely the Jews) was set forth as God's Kingdom purpose from the very beginning of salvation history. He undoubtedly revealed passages like Isaiah 42:6 and 49:6, where God revealed to Isaiah the global dimensions of the salvation work of Messiah.[xxx] The whole idea was this work was to be continued by ordinary, normal, fallible people, empowered and filled by the Holy Spirit's power. Believers were meant to be recipients of the blessings of God who participated in His global purposes. These two realities were never to be separated one from the other as we often find today.

Third, the disciples were told to return to Jerusalem to wait "for the promise of the Father (Acts 1:4)," the coming of the Holy Spirit, empowering them to continue all Jesus did and taught (Acts 1:1). He was helping the disciples prepare for the reality of what He had previously taught them – that He would be taken away from them but the Holy Spirit would come. Thus they were not to do the logical thing - seeking to accomplish the Great Commission in their own strength – but to first go and wait for His coming upon them. Jesus fully understood human nature's tendency to try to accomplish spiritual work through natural means. Instead, Jesus reveals that, in His Kingdom, there is another way. They were to wait for the outpouring of the Spirit, receiving His fullness in their lives (Acts 1:8; John 20:22; Luke 24:49). It is only through the Spirit enabling and empowering believers that true fruit can be produced through our lives and in the Great Commission.

After these 40 days, Jesus ascended into the sky (Mark 16:19; Acts 1:9-11). This supernatural experience was the final mark that He was truly the victorious Son of God. His dramatic departure confirmed the Kingdom He brought near through His life and ministry. It also confirmed He now possessed all authority as He was seated at God's right hand. He was now the Lord of history, to whom every knee would one day bow. His rising from the dead by God the Father, exalted to His right hand, seated forever, also revealed the end of an era. The Kingdom had been brought near through His Person and His work, opening the door for the reconciliation of all humanity and confirming the finality of His atoning sacrifice. The Kingdom reign of the Risen Christ had begun. The initial era had ended in the cross, resurrection and this ascension while the second era would not end until His Kingdom was completely restored through His second coming.

Jesus now reigns through the Holy Spirit within the Church. He is absent in body until His second coming in power and glory. Having been lifted up on the cross, He now draws all humanity to Himself, transferring people from the kingdom of darkness to the Kingdom of God. At present, His Kingdom is outwardly hidden, known only to His people by faith. He looks with heart anticipation for the day when He will return in the same way He departed (Acts 1:11), when every eye will see Him (Revelation 1:4-7) and all His enemies will be put under His feet (1 Corinthians 15:24-26).

Phase One Summary

Phase One of the Gospel of the Kingdom provides foundational understanding of who God is, how all things came into being, humanity's fall into sin, God's plan to bring salvation and restore His Kingdom, and the means through which He does so – the death and resurrection of God in the flesh, Jesus Christ. Let's now consider Phase Two, where the call for a response, change and turning– the result of grasping the sub-truths revealed in Phase One– takes place.

5

PHASE TWO

Born Again Into God's Kingdom

Phase Two of the Gospel of the Kingdom is the part of the *Gospel* we are most familiar. The lost may be awakened to follow Christ through *Phase One* yet not know how to enter His Kingdom. In *Phase One*, we sow seeds of Kingdom truth related to the life and ministry of Christ. In *Phase Two*, we reap a great harvest the Holy Spirit is preparing. In *Phase Two*, we issue God's invitation to come to Him and drink. We see this symbolism both in the Old (Isaiah 55:3) and New Testaments (John 4:13). Jesus offers the only truly satisfying answer to humanity's thirst. Religious expressions continue to leave human beings thirsting for more. They do not satisfy the long-term hunger at the deepest levels of human experience. Jesus is completely unique as He comes to us in love. As we receive Him, He fills us with Himself. We persuade families, households, relatives, friends, co-workers and those in an unreached sub-culture to respond to Jesus' invitation to enter His brought-near Kingdom.

Phase Two of the Gospel of the Kingdom – Human Beings Enter the 'Brought-Near' Kingdom by Being Born Again from Above

The life of the Kingdom of God, realized in fullness at Jesus' second coming, has entered the present age through the life and ministry of Jesus *(Phase One)* so that human beings may be born again from above, entering God's Kingdom *(Phase Two)*. The condition of entering His Kingdom is receiving true inner life from God – receiving His new birth (being born of God) from above.

A. Coming to God on His Terms (John 6:35-40)

A central point of Truth is realizing human beings cannot come to God on their own terms, based on personal, family, cultural or societal ideas and opinions. Every culture is full of concepts of what it means to be spiritual, religious or "good." Following Truth means turning our backs on much of what popular culture esteems and instead buying into what "God in the flesh" – Jesus the Christ – reveals about how human beings were always meant to live in fellowship with God. Even many Christian churches and denominations teach a salvation based on popular sentiments of the day, foreign to the Gospel of the Kingdom and the Bible itself. We want to return to Truth as revealed in Scripture, from the mouth of the Son of God Himself, as this is the only secure and satisfying answer to the mess of our lives and society. Let's consider some of the terms of Jesus related to His Kingdom and living in cooperation with it.

B. We Cannot See the Kingdom of God (John 3:3)

Jesus' first recorded reference to the Kingdom of God is found in John 3:3 as He talks with Nicodemus, *"Verily I say unto you, except one is born again, he cannot see the Kingdom of God."* Nicodemus was a Pharisee who saw something unique in Jesus. He came to Jesus sincerely, wanting to know more about God's will for humanity. Nicodemus knew much about the "Kingdom of God" as this phrase was regularly used in Jewish teaching from the Old Testament.[xxxi] Jesus deliberately connected a concept Nicodemus understood with a new, fresh and mystical twist, confusing him. As King, Jesus knew humanity's condition, separated from God due to inherited sin and its effects. Because of this separation, a person could not see, know or experience the Kingdom of God apart from experiencing a new birth from above.

John reveals about Jesus in John 1:12, *"But as many a received Him, to them He gave the right to become children of God, to those who believe in His name, who were born, not of blood, nor of the will of the flesh, nor the* _will of man, but of God."_ This verse reveals a portion of the incredible inheritance provided and the process of restoration, enabling us to see and experience the Kingdom of God. We become _Children of God._ All human beings experience natural, physical birth, yet believers in Jesus have subsequently experienced something entirely different. They have been born of God, having nothing to do with their blood line, ethnic background or family status/ reputation. Being born of God is entirely separate from who your parents were or what they did. It is entirely brought about because of God's love and perfect knowledge of every human being, desiring to bring them into the very plan and purpose of their existence.

C. What Is the New Birth? (John 3:3)

The Holy Spirit, sent from God, fully God Himself, has come to us in this age to dwell in our hearts. He provides the life of the Kingdom, empowering us to enjoy fellowship with God, as always intended in the heart of God. The Holy Spirit awakens a person's human spirit, and they come into relationship with God in a new way. The experience affects human beings at the deepest part of their lives - life direction is changed, loyalties redefined, and values reoriented. They shift allegiances, having the essence of culturally held beliefs altered. They begin to gather together in spiritual communities that glorify God. This experience is what Jesus termed being "born again," or the "new birth." Another commonly used phrase is "being converted," meaning the same thing. The "new birth" or "conversion" is that great spiritual change indispensable to salvation. Jesus compares this experience to a _birth,_ and because it is essentially alien from our natural birth, He refers to it as a second or new birth. Jesus says in our above verse, John 3:3, _"I tell you the truth, no one can see the kingdom of God unless he is born again"_ - born _over_ again.

The first, or natural, birth introduces human beings to this present world of physical being, thought and feeling. It ushers us into a state of physical existence in which all things are physically new. Between this and the "new birth" there exists a significant resemblance. In the "new birth," the *human spirit* is ushered into a new, spiritual world – *the Kingdom of God*. The "new birth" fashions our spirits to become citizens of the Kingdom. We cannot enter that Kingdom without being born again. Our natural birth ushers us into a world of sin, destruction and eternal death, *the second birth* into a world of holiness, fellowship with God and life as it was intended. It is the birth of the human spirit into grace.

In keeping with our analogy, the new birth is also represented as an awakening, a bringing to life, passing from death to life. Paul describes in Ephesians 2:1, "*And you He made alive, who were dead in trespasses and sins.*" He continues in verses five and six, explaining, "*Even when we were dead in trespasses, made us alive together with Christ (by grace you have been saved), and raised us up together, and made us sit together in the heavenly places in Christ Jesus.*"

The "new birth" is not about religion. Many compare following Jesus to "another religion," yet it is nothing of the sort. The religious expressions of the world are trying to "get to God," helping people do all they can to be acceptable to God. Through the "new birth," we recognize we can never do enough to be acceptable to God. Jesus, God in the flesh, has come near to humanity, providing the only atoning sacrifice available to wash sin, reconciling those who believe to right relationship with Almighty God. We simply receive it. The "new birth" is all about a love relationship with God Himself. The "new birth" is the beginning of the greatest, most exhilarating adventure the human heart and spirit have ever experienced, the beginning of eternal life itself.

D. The Brought-Near Kingdom Is Deliberately Entered (John 3:5)

Jesus states in John 3:5, "*Except a person be born of water and the Spirit, he cannot enter the Kingdom of God.*" Some have wrongly assumed since the King died for the sins of humanity and was raised from the dead, human beings automatically receive the free gift of salvation without taking a step to receive it. These events opened the way for human beings to experience the Kingdom of God, yet deliberate steps must be taken by individuals to enter the available Kingdom.

Jesus treated humanity as being outside the Kingdom of God apart from a deliberate response. They have not yet experienced the new birth (conversion), the supernatural experience of God cleansing the human spirit and indwelling that human spirit with the Holy Spirit. Human beings can do nothing to earn the Kingdom. Instead, we admit our inability to do anything to deserve it, to be worthy of it, simply receiving the King's vast generosity. We embrace the King, receiving His Kingdom.

Jesus was perfectly clear in His teaching about how a person may enter the Kingdom.[xxxii] He announces in John 14:6, *"I am the way, the truth, and the life. No one comes to the Father except through me."* Again, in John 10:9 and 11, He reveals, *"I am the door. If anyone enters by Me, he will be saved, and will go in and out and find pasture. ... I am the good shepherd. The good shepherd gives His life for the sheep."* Human beings enter the Kingdom of God only through Jesus. There is no other suitable mediator between God and humanity except God in the flesh, Jesus Christ. Jesus confirms this in a clear and conclusive statement in John 6:40: *"And this is the will of Him who sent Me, that everyone who sees the Son and believes in Him may have everlasting life; and I will raise him up at the last day."*

E. The Kingdom Demands a Decision (Acts 16:31)

Paul revealed in Romans 10:9, *"If you confess with your lips that Jesus is Lord and believe in your heart that God raised Him from the dead, you will be saved."* He tells the Philippian jailer in Acts 16:31, *"Believe in the Lord Jesus and you will be saved."* From these verses have come a variety of formulas and creeds. Is the Kingdom entered by merely taking Jesus' name on our lips? Is God interested primarily in a verbal confession? Can the speaking of certain phrases save a person?

What does "Jesus is Lord" mean?

These Scriptures refer to the primary demand the Kingdom of God makes upon human beings – a decision of the will, a revolution within. The Kingdom demands a turning around, reversing the course of life, a changing of direction, embracing the Kingdom of God. The foundational response to the Kingdom of God is to receive it, yield to it.[xxxiii] In Christ, the Kingdom of God now confronts us. In *Phase Two*, Jesus is putting before all human beings a decision of their will based on the facts revealed in *Phase One*.

F. A Thorough and Steadfast Decision (Luke 9:57-62)

This decision of the will cannot be taken lightly. It must be a thorough, steadfast decision. In Luke 9:57-62, Jesus relates with three people about this serious, thorough and steadfast decision.[xxxiv] The first man seemed ready to follow Jesus. Jesus tells him in v. 58, *"Foxes have holes, birds of the air have nests, but the Son of Man has nowhere to lay His head."* Jesus is testing his seriousness. Are you willing to become a homeless disciple, with no social status? Have you adequately thought this through, considered its implications?

The second man tells Jesus in v. 59, *"Lord, let me first go bury my father."* It sounds fairly harmless and honoring to his father. Yet Jesus sees through it, recognizing he was ready to follow but wanted to wait a bit. He had good intentions but wanted time to deal with other, seemingly more important things. The Kingdom of God demands immediate action without waiting around for a future, good time to follow.

A third man declares in v. 61, *"Lord I will follow you but first let me say farewell to those at my home."* This again seems reasonable. Here was a man professing willingness yet being reluctant. Jesus responds that there is no place for reluctance, hesitation, no turning back. The decision for the Kingdom is to be all or nothing. People are not to hold onto their old lives. Jesus states in v. 62, *"No one who puts his* hand to the plough and looks back *is fit for the Kingdom.*" The Kingdom demands a thorough and complete decision.

G. A Radical Decision (Matthew 11:12; Luke 16:16)

In addition, the Kingdom requires a radical decision. Jesus teaches the demand of the Kingdom is like that of violence and force.[xxxv] In Matthew 11:12, He describes it this way: *"From the days of John the Baptist until now the Kingdom of heaven works mightily and men of violence take it by force."* He further clarifies in Luke 16:16 by adding, *"The law and the prophets were until John, since then the good news of the Kingdom of God is preached and every one enters it violently."* The idea of violence related to the Kingdom of God sounds strange.

Jesus uses metaphorical language in the Gospels to push a consistent idea – the demand of radical decision. Some of this language is included in Mark 9:47: *"If your eye causes you to sin, pluck it out. It is better to enter the Kingdom of God with one eye rather than having two eyes and be cast into hell fire."* A violent thought indeed! Again, in Matthew 10:34, Jesus announces, *"Do not think I came to bring peace on the earth. I have not come to bring peace but a sword."* Sometimes, decisions for the Kingdom will demand radical commitment that cuts across close relations, even family units. The imagery communicates the call to a radical, wholehearted decision for the Kingdom because Jesus is so entirely worth it.

H. A Costly Decision (Galatians 2:20)

The Kingdom demands a costly decision. Jesus clarifies in Matthew 10:38, *"He who does not take up His cross and follow me is not worthy of me."* In Matthew 16:24, He reveals the same concept using slightly different words: *"If any one desires to come after Me, let him deny himself and take us his cross and follow Me. For whoever desires to save his life will lose it, but whoever loses his life for my sake will find it."* Taking up one's cross means a readiness to die with and for Christ.

It is giving our all to Jesus – our will, ambitions, plans, desires and hopes. I consider myself dead and my life alive in Christ that He may reign in and through me. Paul describes the essence of this costly decision in Galatians 2:20: *"I have been crucified with Christ, it is no longer I who live, but Christ who lives in me."*

Taking up our cross is a foundational element in a believer's relationship with Jesus. It relates to Jesus' Lordship and Kingship over us. There can only be one King in my life – either myself or Jesus. By embracing the cross, I am welcoming Jesus to rule and reign as King and Lord over all my life. I am no longer in control, free to do as I want or choose. I am His bond-slave, willingly surrendered in love.

I. We Come As We Are (Romans 5:8)

The "new birth" does not mean a person has complete understanding of their new faith, having all their doctrine lined up, but marks the beginning of a lifetime adventure of growing in relationship with Jesus. The Kingdom does not demand we find in ourselves the righteousness it requires before we enter. Human beings, apart from Jesus, have nothing to offer God. We have no righteousness that counts before God. Instead, we receive from God the righteousness of His Kingdom as we enter it and walk according to its ways. We lay down pride, trying to make ourselves good enough for God, instead receiving His perfect righteousness as a free gift. He then changes our lives as we align with His values and will. God does not require us to live according to a certain standard before we enter His Kingdom. Instead, we receive His supernatural enabling to walk out His biblically defined standards. We come before Him humbly in our nothingness, receiving His all. This is the beginning of life in His Kingdom.

J. The Result of a Process

The "new birth" experience is the result of a process taking place within a person's heart and mind that prepares them for this radical decision of the will. The "new birth" does not take place in a vacuum. Moving from "darkness" to "light" and confessing Jesus as Lord of one's life, apart from a series of outside influences on the life, is not likely or common. We do not see people coming to faith in Jesus in this way in Scripture. Instead, we find God dealing with a group or individuals in a purposeful and unique way. God is working in their situations during the "discipling" phase of the Gospel. This is the period before people make a public decision to take Jesus as Lord of their lives. During this time, they are experiencing a variety of forms of "awareness" of truth about who God is, what He has done, and what it means to follow Him. In addition, factors producing awareness are not necessarily spiritual in nature. Many natural situations, either influencing groups or individuals (such as economic changes, pressures, crises, etc.) are used by God to make people "aware" of God and His teachings. In these circumstances, a new option is presented to help people facing problems and needing solutions. The message bearer is often the advocate for change providing the needed awareness, bringing the group or person to the point of experiencing the "new birth."

K. The Righteousness of God (Romans 3:21-22)

It is absolutely necessary to grasp the revelation of God's righteousness to experience the Gospel of the Kingdom. The righteousness of God means the very quality of God's righteousness has been freely given to all sinners who repent and come to Jesus in faith. Paul declared in Romans 1:17, *"For in it [the gospel of the Kingdom] the righteousness of God is revealed from faith to faith."* In Jesus, a completely new reality has been made available – *"Now the righteousness of God apart from the law [earning it] is revealed... (Rom. 3:21)."*

There are two expressions of God's righteousness, imputed and imparted. The moment we are born again, He gives us the gift of righteousness to empower us to live righteously. This is **_imputed_** righteousness, which gives us a new **_legal position_** before God (Romans 3-5); it is instantaneous. God also gives us **_imparted_** righteousness, which describes our **_living condition_** before God (Romans 6-8). This happens progressively, as we live in agreement with God and actively *"live according to the Spirit"* (Rom. 8:5) and *"put to death the deeds of the body"* (Rom. 8:13), living according to His will.

Paul elaborates on the way of salvation by emphasizing how God's justice is involved in giving us the gift of righteousness (Rom. 3:21-31). By understanding God's justice, we realize that *all* can be saved, that we can stand *confidently before God*, and that we can be kept from the error of believing that there is *another way of salvation*, outside of Jesus paying the debt for our sin.[xxxvi]

L. No Trusting In 'Goodness' (Philippians 3:7-9)

Paul provides a significant caution by using his own experience in Philippians 3:7-9: *"But what things were gain to me, these I have counted loss for Christ. Yet indeed I also count all things loss for the excellence of the knowledge of Christ Jesus my Lord...and be found in Him, not having my own righteousness, which is from the law, but that which is through faith in Christ, the righteousness which is from God by faith."*

We do not rely on anything we think makes us "good" before God. Like Paul, we count these things "loss," meaning we recognize that within ourselves or through achievements, accolades, education, heritage, or families, there is nothing that can "save" us before a holy God. Conversely, no lack in our lives excludes us from His Kingdom. His righteousness alone is the basis of our coming before God in faith.

For those from a Muslim, Buddhist or Hindu background, it is necessary to overcome various religious rituals done to "earn" one's salvation through merit-making in all its forms or thinking that religious observance can "save." Nothing we do can make us acceptable to God. Only taking the work of His Son, through His death and resurrection, receiving the un-earned, free gift of God's righteousness on our behalf as our own, are we born again.

M. Laying Down Logic and Intellect (Isaiah 55:9)

Receiving new life from God is experienced as human beings suspend natural and logical thinking, embracing the upside-down nature of God, His Kingdom and His ways. He is completely *Other*. His thoughts and ways are beyond those of human beings. Many seek to figure out God and His ways using the natural mind. When certain areas remain a mystery, they conclude these things can't be right or real. It is a mistake for the created ones, in our finite capacities, to assume we are able to grasp the infinite mysteries of Creator God. We do not receive the new birth through intellectual concepts or the experience of our five senses but by evidence experienced in our hearts and seen in Creation, producing belief and faith. A person becomes a follower of Jesus, experiencing the "new birth," when their heart first reaches out in faith to their new Lord. Their surrender may not be strong, yet it is real nonetheless. God sees and affirms it, receiving the person into the household of faith at that moment.

N. Experiencing Eternal Life – the Knowledge of God (John 17:3)

By receiving the new birth, human beings receive the free gift of eternal life. Eternal life generally refers to the Kingdom of God in the age to come. Yet, as we've seen, eternal life has invaded this present age through the Kingdom of God coming near through Jesus' first coming. We can now experience eternal life in the present, in the midst of death and decay all around us.

What is eternal life? Jesus describes it vividly in John 17:3: *"And this is eternal life that they may know You, the only true God, and Jesus Christ whom you have sent."* Eternal life is experiential knowledge of the Father and Son. The word "know" does not refer to mere head facts about God, nor certain doctrines, reciting a creed or knowing a few Bible verses. Knowledge means experiencing God, referring to personal relationship and fellowship. Knowing a person means entering a mutual friendship of closeness and fellowship. We experience "eternal life" now with the assurance that, in the future Kingdom of God, our fellowship and experiential knowledge of God will be perfected through being face to face. We have already begun to enter that life while looking to its full establishment in the future. Our present fellowship with the Father and Son will be wonderfully enlarged in the future Kingdom of God.

Our understanding of truth and its application to life will also be enlarged. When we receive perfect knowledge of God in the future Kingdom, we will grasp God's complete truth in ways beyond current comprehension. We shall be taught of God Himself. God, according to His purpose, has allowed us to experience a measure of divine truth now, yet Paul clarifies in 1 Corinthians 13:12, *"For now we see in a mirror, dimly, but then face to face. Now I know in part, but then I shall know just as I am also known."* Ancient mirrors were not like what we have today. They were made of metal and easily tarnished, providing an imperfect image. We experience truth now but are humble before God and others, realizing we "know in part" without yet having the full picture.

O. Experiencing Eternal Life – the Indwelling Holy Spirit (Ephesians 1:13-14)

In 2 Corinthians 5:5, Paul clarifies, *"Now He who has prepared us for this very thing is God, who also has given us the Spirit as a guarantee."* In a similar vein, He teaches in Ephesians 1:13-14, *"In whom also, having believed, you were sealed with the Holy Spirit of promise, who is the guarantee of our inheritance until the redemption of the purchased possession, to the praise of His glory."* The inheritance Paul mentions is the redemption of the body, from our flesh-and-blood bodies into the fullness of strength, power and glory of spiritual bodies. This inheritance is waiting for us in the future Kingdom, while in the present God has given the Holy Spirit to dwell in us as a guarantee of the yet-future inheritance.

The present indwelling Holy Spirit is the partial down payment of the full possession of our spiritual bodies at the coming of the future Kingdom when Jesus returns. The new birth into the present Kingdom is the beginning of eternal life. It is partial in the present age and yet as real as it will be in the coming fullness. Believers experiencing the new birth already have the life of heaven within, already participating in the life belonging to God's future Kingdom.

Through the miracle of the "new birth," the Holy Spirit has indwelled our human spirit, making it new. The Holy Spirit lives in a person in a real, personal and individual way. He is actively present in every believer, no matter how new a believer they might be. It is not an overstatement to say a follower of Jesus is one who has the living Spirit of Jesus within. The new believer leaves the old life of self-centered focus and begins to experience life under the leadership of the Holy Spirit (Romans 8:9).

A believer's new life in Christ is only possible because of the indwelling Spirit. This is more than the forgiveness of sins, more than acceptance before a holy God. It is a person vitally unified with the true God through the Holy Spirit. God interacts with the believer at a deep, spiritual level, impacting the essence of their being. It is the presence of the Holy Spirit in every believer's life that is central to growing into the disciple God intends them to be. He is their teacher, instructor, the one who guides them into all truth and spiritual understanding.

Pastors, message bearers and other spiritual leaders must learn to trust the Holy Spirit to teach new believers. We hinder their development if we do all their thinking and teaching for them. Paul believed the Holy Spirit would instruct and guide new believers as they are now sons and daughters of God with heavy responsibility in His Kingdom. Recent believers are expected to live according to the standard God laid out when He called them (Ephesians 4:1), to live like people belonging to the light (Ephesians 5:8). This is only possible as they learn to rely on the Holy Spirit and not only on their spiritual leaders. This is true no matter how much background they might or might not have in biblical truth.

P. Making Jesus Lord (1 Corinthians 8:5-6)

Receiving the "new birth" means a change in allegiance and loyalty. Paul says in 1 Corinthians 8:6, *"Yet for us there is one God, the Father, of whom are all things, and one Lord Jesus Christ... ."* When a human being experiences new life, traditional allegiances are forsaken and Jesus becomes the center of the new life. The new believer is now able to live out the Truth that "Jesus is Lord" (1 Corinthians 12:3). Jesus will have preeminence in the new life given over to Him (Colossians 1:18). This does not mean former gods and spirits are no longer real. Instead, Jesus' power is greater than traditional gods, stronger then the spirit world. Jesus is the one God, worthy to rule over our lives with absolute authority as Lord. We crown Him King of our lives, submitting our desires and worship to Him alone. Making Jesus Lord reveals a person has experienced the "new birth." Day by day, as a new believer learns about themselves, growing in Jesus, they surrender more to God's control, leadership and ways.

Q. Becoming One With Christ (Galatians 3:26-28; 1 Corinthians 1:30)

New believers do not merely put another level of teaching onto one's previous religious experience. They do not simply add Jesus into the mix of other gods, idols and spiritual loyalties. By faith, a believer enters a living relationship with the one true God, becoming one with Him through Jesus. We experience "union life" (Galatians 3:27) with Jesus and are now *"clothed with the life of Jesus Christ Himself."*

Paul consistently talks in His letters about this new relationship and its closeness. Born-again believers are *"in Christ,"* a phrase Paul highlights 72 times, referring to the spiritual relationship we now enjoy with our Lord.[xxxvii] It is a relationship unbound by time and space, able to be experienced everywhere due to His powerful presence. Our whole lives are to be governed by this relationship – all actions, behaviors and attitudes. *"In Christ,"* He becomes the standard of life. We relate differently with other believers as we are all together *"in Christ,"* part of His global body. This oneness with Christ enables new believers to discern right from wrong as they allow Him to teach them in each unique situation.

R. Progress in the Right Direction (2 Corinthians 3:18)

The "new birth" does not mean a new believer's outward life will automatically begin to look like every other believer. The nature of the Kingdom of God as the rule and reign over one's life is progressive. The Kingdom means new believers will seek to be obedient to God. They deliberately choose to set their heart toward obedience, though they still make mistakes. They quickly confess these, continuing to press on toward obedience to God and His ways. There is joy in their new faith while the struggle with the old life continues. A believer makes clear progress from what they have been over time. Paul revealed the life of faith as "discernible progress in the right direction."[xxxviii]

Paul referred to all believers (new and older believers) as "saints." He did not mean this primarily about their behavior but as referring to their spiritual standing before God. Paul expected believers to see one another through the lens of the "Spirit" and not the "flesh." By seeing each other "in the Spirit," we take the perspective of what God has done in us and what others can be in Christ. Viewing them "according to the flesh" means we negatively focus on their flaws, disobediences and how they fall short of Christ's standard. Paul could call the Corinthian new believers "saints," though they were not yet walking according to all of Jesus' ways. The Corinthian believers were sincerely moving in this direction but were not there yet.

S. Sharing Life in Community (Ephesians 1:22-23)

The people of the Kingdom share a new togetherness as joint members of the body of Christ, the living Church of Jesus Christ, a living, global, united community of faith. This global community is made up of born-again believers from every nationality, economic background and social status. They possess a common, mutual life within the context of individual participation in Jesus Christ. This is the mystery of the Church. It is a supernatural, spiritual community bound together through union with Jesus by the Holy Spirit.

It is necessary for every believer to join a local body of believers, a local church. It is through the conduit of this spiritual family that new believers grow and mature as true disciples, laying hold of the sub-truths of the next three phases of the Gospel of the Kingdom. It is through the community of worship, prayer, encouragement, teaching and equipping for ministry that spiritual strength is released to live faithfully for the Kingdom of God. Here, they grow in grace and experiential knowledge of Jesus Christ.

The community expresses itself through corporate worship, mutual sharing, united confession, and service to others. A local church is characterized by steadfast commitment to apostolic teaching and application of the Word of God, sharing of the sacraments (the Lord's Supper), life-on-life vulnerability and fellowship, and a lifestyle of devoted intercession (Acts 2:42) undergirding the life of the community. The community protects their corporate holiness through deliberately dealing with sin in their midst, not merely pushing it under the carpet (Acts 5:1-6). Churches are permanent centers of fellowship, worship, training and outreach for a local community of followers of Jesus.

The global Church of Christ is a divine concept yet filled with flawed individuals saved by grace. In this age, the visible body of Christ will always be a mixture of purity and brokenness, the wheat of the power of the Holy Spirit and the tares of demonic manipulation (Matthew 13:24-30). The Church realizes its potential when the powerful presence of Jesus is given greater freedom and rule within the body.

T. Receiving Baptism (Romans 6:3-4)

The biblical byproduct of becoming born-again is receiving baptism. The book of Acts reveals no un-baptized believers within the early churches. Each of the five recorded conversions In Acts included baptism (8:36-38; 10:47-48; 9:18; 22:16; 16:15; 16:33). Baptism followed quickly after decisions were made to take Jesus as Lord, not weeks or months later.

It is seemingly not a biblical practice to withhold baptism from new believers as has been the practice of many mission organizations and churches. Baptism represented the public confession of a new believer's repentance and faith, confirming saving faith. There is little evidence in Scripture that baptism is a "reward" for study, literacy, class attendance or being able to answer certain doctrinal questions. Several of those converted in the Acts accounts would not have been able to answer much about the new faith yet were baptized almost immediately. Baptism is the first step of discipleship (**Acts 8:26-39**), symbolizing thorough commitment, no going back. In the New Testament, it was understood a believer not taking this step remained uncommitted.

Baptism is related to the gift of the indwelling Holy Spirit (not to be confused with the filling of the Spirit). This gift is the crucial element in becoming born again from above as it reveals God's acceptance of the individual and group. Baptism then becomes the believers' acknowledgement of that acceptance by God. As baptism is ministered in the name of the Father, Son and Holy Spirit, God now fully owns the individual or family. Baptism is an initiation into the dynamic, ongoing life of the global body of Christ. It provides incorporation into the new community of faith in Jesus, necessary for new believers coming out of old communities that may be hostile to the person/ family choosing to follow Jesus.

Baptism is an outward act symbolizing the inward transformation of receiving Jesus Christ as the sacrificial means reconciling us to God. It signifies death to the old life and the old world order that is passing away. A new believer is now a part of the new world order, the Kingdom of God, with its power activated in their lives, though this Kingdom power is often hidden from others.

Baptism looks to the death and resurrection of Jesus, being brought into union with Christ, identifying a believer with His work. Just as Christ died and was buried, so the baptized believer is submerged under water. And just as Christ rose again from beneath the earth, so the baptized person rises again from beneath the water. Under the water, the believer's old, dead, heavy life remains. Out of the water, cleansed by the blood of Christ, is the believer's new, fresh, vibrant, victorious life.

Summary of Phase Two

We have seen the power of *Phase Two* of the Gospel of the Kingdom. Unbelievers cross from the Kingdom of darkness to light, receiving a "new birth" from God, becoming born again, receiving the gift of the indwelling Spirit. They are baptized and brought into the community of faith. At this point, it is all too common new believers are left to fend for themselves. Yet, the Gospel of the Kingdom proceeds, having much more to provide these new believers, establishing them on solid ground. The Holy Spirit is committed to leading millions of new believers into maturity in Jesus. *Phase Three* lays crucial groundwork to growing in that spiritual maturity.

6
PHASE THREE
The Blessings, Benefits and Privileges
of the Kingdom

Phase Three of the Gospel of the Kingdom is largely overlooked as we focus efforts on getting unreached peoples "saved." It is through *Phase Three* that new believers, having received the new birth, grow into disciples. In this phase, believers receive and apply the vastness of their spiritual inheritance in the Kingdom of God. The word *disciple* occurs in the New Testament 269 times, while *believer* is used only twice. Jesus' will is that those experiencing the new birth progress to becoming true, mature disciples. Obviously, a disciple must be a believer, but according to Jesus, not all believers are disciples.

We receive the new birth from God in *Phase Two*, choosing a new path, receiving Jesus' death and resurrection as our penalty before a holy God. We make a deliberate, thorough, steadfast, radical and costly decision for His Kingdom. We join a local church, connecting to a local expression of the global body of Christ, and receive baptism.

Regrettably, many new believers remain at *Phase Two* without progressing to maturity in Christ. They are born-again, living in the Kingdom, yet not actively engaged with growing into the disciple God intended. This is often no fault of their own as many have not been taught about becoming a mature disciple. In *Phase Three*, we grasp and apply the benefits, blessings and privileges made available through the Kingdom of God. They are the inheritance Jesus purchased for His body through His death and resurrection, meant to be applied toward His Kingdom purposes in this age. Over a lifetime, we experience these in consistently deepening ways, making them our own, demonstrating their power to others.

Phase Three of the Gospel of the Kingdom – Those Entering the Kingdom Receive All the Benefits, Blessings and Privileges of Their New Inheritance

Paul affirms in Ephesians 2:19, *"You (those born again from above) are no longer strangers and foreigners, but fellow citizens with the saints and members of the household of God..."* All born-again peoples are welcomed in the "household of God," equal in value before the King. There are no castes, economic classes or sub-categories in His Kingdom. No superior, majority peoples and conversely no oppressed minorities. Life in the Kingdom aligns with the King's values, pitting us against what He hates – oppressing and exploiting others, injustices, racism, false superiority, devaluing anyone who is different, trafficking in all its forms, taking power over others in any form, murder, abortion and more.

Jesus promises, *"Fear not, little flock; for it is your Father's good pleasure to give you the Kingdom"* (Luke 12:32). Paul goes on to say in Ephesians 1:3, *"Blessed be the God and Father of our Lord Jesus Christ, who has blessed us with every spiritual blessing in the heavenly places in Christ..."* Both Jesus and Paul clarify the degree God is willing to go in giving His children all that is available in His Kingdom. These verses reveal all believers are given a metaphorical banqueting table in God's Kingdom, full of the most wonderful foods. Yet, a banqueting table must be partaken of. We don't merely look at the sumptuous foods but dig in, enjoying them to the fullest. God has made every spiritual blessing available, but it is our choice to what extent we experience them. We must receive and apply them. Apart from doing so, we will not grow spiritually mature.

Aware of Satan's Schemes

A major factor in believers failing to effectively partake of the spiritual blessings of the Kingdom is Satan's incessant accusations against believers. In Revelation 12:10, John declares, *"Then I heard a loud voice saying in heaven, 'Now salvation, and strength, and the*

Kingdom of our God, and the power of His Christ have come, for the accuser of our brethren, who accused them before our God day and night, has been cast down.'" This event happens at the return of Christ. In this present age, Satan accuses (or lies to us), putting false ideas in our minds about ourselves, others, God and the Kingdom. A primary lie is getting us to believe we are disqualified before God because of failures and mistakes. We subtly start to believe God's blessings and benefits aren't available to us.

Satan sows five false measuring sticks that get us off track in God: (1) How badly we are treated; (2) how hard things are; (3) what we do not have; (4) how much we fail; and (5) how worthless our life is. He wants the narrative in our minds to revolve around several of these at any given time. If these five dominate our thoughts, we will have difficulty walking in our inheritance. Satan sows these just enough so we draw back, not applying ourselves to the spiritual blessings of our inheritance. Instead, we fight the false narrative with truths of God related to us. We rise in faith, resisting deceptions, taking hold of *every* spiritual blessing God has provided through Jesus Christ.

The Kingdom inheritance of *Phase Three* is primarily not for ourselves but extending the Kingdom of God on earth. God wants us enjoying Him and the blessings immensely. However, some receive these blessings, benefits and privileges with a self-centered motive. Using them for themselves reveals a heart failing to *"seek first the Kingdom of God"*(Matthew 6:33). We lift our eyes to see the big picture of the unfolding of history and the drama God is bringing forth. Failing to lay hold of these areas of inheritance hinders the flow of resources meant to aid in extending the Kingdom among all peoples.

Laying Hold of Our Inheritance

In Romans 1:16, Paul explodes with a glorious truth: *"I am not ashamed of the gospel of Christ, for it is the power of God to salvation for everyone who believes!"* The Kingdom releases the power of God in human experience when we believe it, applying its truths to everyday circumstances and situations. There is no distinction of races, genders, education, etc. *Everyone* can experience Kingdom power in their circumstances. The only condition is we "believe." This refers to more than "believing" when we were first born-again. What Paul means is daily "believing" in God's power to release His Kingdom privileges into our circumstances. The power of the Gospel is experienced in an ongoing, growing way through active "believing" in Him as we face life's situations.

A crucial aspect of the life of faith is receiving from God. The degree we experience the areas of inheritance will be limited to the extent we actively, consistently receive. Paul in Philippians 3:12 provided a key for this phase of the Gospel of the Kingdom. *"Not that I have already attained, or am already perfected; but I press on, that I may lay hold of that for which Christ Jesus has also laid hold of me."* Jesus has made all aspects of His Kingdom available to born-again believers. Yet, we have a role in obtaining them. *We lay hold of them.* Many believers passively relate with their Kingdom inheritance. God has already made all aspects available. We, therefore, actively receive them into our situations by faith. We cannot earn them, we merely receive them. With each of the many benefits of the Kingdom in *Phase Three*, we open our hearts to receive. We apply and lay hold of each one, guiding other believers to do so as well, making them our own through experience.

Let's consider a range of crucial benefits, blessings and privileges made available to every born-again believer in the global body of Jesus Christ.

A. First-Class Citizens of the Kingdom (Colossians 1:12)

No matter where you are from, what family you come from, the education you have, or the status you possess in the world, because of Jesus' death and resurrection, God declares believers first-class citizens of His Kingdom. This is difficult to comprehend for those from minority ethnic peoples who are oppressed and subjugated in the world's systems. In Jesus' Kingdom, all are equal, valuable, possessing eternal significance and worth. Having eternal value and worth, we have restored dignity through God's love for us. God restores honor and true identity as children of the King, with all shame removed.

Jesus reveals in John 15:16, *"You did not choose Me, but I chose you and appointed you that you should go and bear fruit, and that your fruit should remain."* We are His through His vast work. Over time, he has brought us to know who He is and what He has done. We marvel at the goodness of God revealing Himself to us, showing us the error of our ways.

God is not mad at us, even when we fail. It cost Him everything (His Son) to make these benefits and privileges available. We are no longer citizens of the world but of His glorious Kingdom. This Kingdom status happened the moment we believed Jesus is the Son of God who paid the penalty for our waywardness. Many believers do not necessarily "feel" this status, giving up on its truth. We speak truth over our hearts and minds, whether we feel it or not. In time, our emotions will begin to experience it more.

B. Adopted, Accepted, Redeemed and Forgiven (Colossians 1:13-18)

No matter our earthly family situation, Creator God, as loving Father, has adopted us into His eternal family. As King, He has every right to *adopt* us as His own when we embrace His Kingdom (Ephesians 1:5). He is the best Father the human heart has ever known, perfectly gentle, kind, encouraging and protective. We are His beloved.

He declares we are *accepted* in Him. No matter what we've done, lifestyles we've had or areas of brokenness we've experienced, if we forsake them, embracing Jesus and His ways, God *accepts* us as righteous because of Jesus' own righteousness (Ephesians 1:6). He is overjoyed with lavish affection and acceptance of us, filled with pleasure because we have believed in and loved His Son.

Being _redeemed_ means we are no longer under God's wrath due to the separation of sin. Jesus, through His own blood, has purchased us back to the Father, destroying the wall between us and God. This is what redeemed literally means – bought back (Ephesians 1:7). If we believe Jesus took the penalty of our sin upon Himself at the cross, God's wrath is now fully satisfied as it was transferred to Jesus.

Forgiven means when we sincerely tell God, "I have missed the mark, made a mistake" in some area, "forgive me," that thing is forgotten by Jesus as His blood covers it (Ephesians 1:7). Sin is no longer accounted against us. Psalm 103:11-12 confirms this: _"For as the heavens are high above the earth, so great is His mercy toward those who fear Him; As far as the east is from the west, so far has He removed our transgressions from us."_ There may be real human consequences of that choice, yet before the throne of God our slate is wiped clean in relation to that thing.

These elements of truth together mean God openly and freely relates with us without any barrier to the relationship. All separation between us and God has been done away with through Jesus' death and resurrection.

C. Experiencing a New Identity (Philippians 3:9)

Part of our inheritance is our identity shifting from what we do, who recognizes us, what strata of society we are from, or how important our family is to being sons and daughters of the living God. Identity is a crucial part of the human makeup: Which ethnic people we belong to, our social and economic class, how we derive importance, what gives us value and worth. These all feed into how we fit into the world, view ourselves and are viewed by others. When we become born-again, a needed adjustment takes place. The source of our previous identity begins to shift, becoming rooted in the right place. We no longer are defined by the myriad of ways the world identifies us. In Jesus, we are sons and daughters of the King, loved and enjoyed by Him, supremely valued. We define ourselves not by external measuring sticks but with the fact of being first-class citizens based in His love. That citizenship is no longer bound by worldly understandings. A misplaced identity causes us to strive, manipulate, scheme and be dishonest. Our identity as a child of God empowers us to overcome when difficulties arise or when someone hurts us.

D. New Creations in Christ (2 Corinthians 5:17, 21)

In 2 Corinthians 5:17, Paul makes a staggering statement that at first looks like an exaggeration: *"Therefore, if anyone is in Christ, he is a new creation; old things have passed away; behold, all things have become new."* What did Paul mean by this? Our spirit has become brand new by Jesus redeeming us from inner destruction while our natural, physical selves remain. We continue to fight our human nature yet now as a *"new creation"* possess spiritual power to overcome because of the indwelling Holy Spirit. Paul is not talking about our physical self or personalities becoming new, but *all things* related to our inner man (or spirit) made new in Christ.

In verse 21, Paul goes on to state, *"For He made Him who knew no sin to become sin for us that we might become the righteousness of God in Him."* We've been forgiven of sin with the righteousness of God imparted to our human spirit. This means we have *become* the righteousness of God. Our spirits have been transferred to a state having no corruption, deemed holy before God. All this happened the day we were born again. Apart from this, the Holy Spirit could not dwell within us. This is what it means to be *"a new creation in Christ."* None of this is reliant on feelings, emotions or even awareness of what has happened. It is a huge piece of the inheritance we've received as sons and daughters of the Kingdom.

This truth was hard for the early church in the book of Acts to understand. In the Old Testament, God did not dwell within human beings. Jews could experience the Holy Spirit "coming upon them." However, He did not live inside of them, making their spirits new. This experience belongs solely to the New Covenant. It provides direct access to the Spirit while empowering us in a way never available in the Old Testament.

E. Alive in Jesus (Ephesians 2:1-3)

Jesus has awakened our spirits, previously dead, and through Him they have been made alive. It is a similar idea of our becoming a "new creation" yet using a different metaphor of a real exchange. *"The old is dead"* and now we have experienced a resurrected spiritual life. Paul says in Romans 6:8, *"If we have died with Christ we shall also live with Him."* A new believer is now alive to God in the same way that Jesus was made alive to God through the resurrection. We have been put to death with Jesus so that Christ may now live in us.

Paul clarifies, *"And you He made alive, who were dead in trespasses and sins, in which you once walked according to the course of this world, according to the prince of the power of the air, the spirit who now works in the sons of disobedience."* Satan is influencing human beings to live in disobedience to God. Yet, Jesus has made us alive in Him, no longer walking according to the disobedient ways of the world. We used to walk in those same ways and, if it were not for the enabling of God, we still would be living that way. Now we can choose another path, God's path according to His will. God intervened, revealed Himself, and we responded with love. Now, we are alive in Him, free to turn our backs on the ways of this world, living a completely different way.

F. Delivered From Darkness (Colossians 1:13)

As born-again believers, we are free from the captivity and dominion of Satan as the full property of the Kingdom of the Son of God's love. No longer our own (1 Corinthians 6:20), living for ourselves, we have been bought at the price of His blood, transferred into His Kingdom, belonging to Him for His glory and purpose alone. Satan can and does attack us, but now we have Kingdom weapons to defeat destructive assignments against us (2 Corinthians 10:4). We actively use these weapons so that we are not vulnerable to the enemy. We live on a different plane than before, no longer slaves to Satan, sin and spiritual darkness, now slaves of righteousness. Our ambitions and desires are laid at His feet in exchange for the more fulfilling desires of His own heart in our lives.

Believers have been delivered from the power of inordinate fears of the spirit world that once gripped us. Many peoples are coming to faith in Jesus out of animist and spiritist backgrounds. This includes folk religious elements of Islam, Buddhism and Hinduism. Fear of demonic spirits, and their backlash against believers, is real. Through Jesus' authority, we help believers recognize His superiority, standing in truth when the spirits seek to do harm. 1 John 4:4 says, *"You are of God, little children, and have overcome them, because He who is in you is greater than he who is in the world."*

G. Conformed to the Likeness of Christ (Matthew 5; Galatians 5)

God's greatest purpose is conforming believers into the likeness of Jesus. This is one of His top priorities. Being conformed to Jesus' likeness means deliberately taking on the values and ways of Jesus and His Kingdom. We learn them, applying them to our circumstances, aligning our thoughts, motives, behaviors and actions with His. This includes aligning our lives with God's intended purposes and plans both in this present age and the age to come.

Jesus is working to form our character and responses, orchestrating situations tailored to forming, shaping and pruning us, establishing His own ways and values within. He lovingly cultivates our hearts to become like His own. In Matthew 5, in Jesus' Sermon on the Mount,

He lays out eight "beatitudes," or characteristics, He primarily values in disciples. These eight are a depiction of Jesus with each one revealing a particular aspect of what Jesus is like. Growing in each of these eight characteristics is one way Jesus forms us into His likeness. Another is by lovingly provoking us to produce the fruit of the Spirit revealed in Galatians 5. These nine attributes are the outflow of a life being conformed to the likeness of Jesus.

H. The Consistent Filling of the Holy Spirit (Ephesians 5:18)

Every born-again believer has received the gift of the indwelling Holy Spirit. The Holy Spirit now dwells within the human spirit. This is a glorious fact as God, the Holy Spirit, has taken up residence within us. Yet, there is another, equally amazing stage of embracing the Holy Spirit necessary to live according to God's ways in the present Kingdom. All believers *have* the Holy Spirit but might not be *filled* with the Holy Spirit. The Bible distinguishes between these two.

In Acts 18:25-26, we meet Apollos. *"This man had been instructed in the way of the Lord; and being fervent in spirit, he spoke and taught accurately the things of the Lord, though he knew only the baptism of John. So he began to speak boldly in the synagogue. When Aquila and Priscilla heard him, they took him aside and explained to him the way of God more accurately."*

The book of Acts differentiates the "baptism of John" with the "baptism of the Spirit." Jesus instructed the disciples who had already received the "baptism of John" in Acts 1:4-6, *"And being assembled together with them, He commanded them not to depart from Jerusalem, but to wait for the Promise of the Father,* "which," He said, "you have heard from Me, *for John truly baptized with water, but you shall be baptized with the Holy Spirit not many days from now."* Later, in Acts 11:16, after the first Gentiles (Cornelius and his household) came to faith and were filled with the Spirit, Peter recalls Jesus' same words as above: *"Then I remembered the word of the Lord, how He said, 'John indeed baptized with water, but you shall be baptized with the Holy Spirit.' "*

Paul highlights a similar experience with believers in Ephesus in Acts 19:1-6. *"And finding some disciples he said to them, "Did you receive the Holy Spirit when you believed? So they said to him, "We have not so much as heard whether there is a Holy Spirit." And he said to them, "Into what then were you baptized? So they said, "Into John's baptism." Then Paul said, "John indeed baptized with a baptism of repentance, saying to the people that they should believe on Him who would come after him, that is, on Christ Jesus. When they heard this, they were baptized in the name of the Lord Jesus. And when Paul had laid hands on them, the Holy Spirit came upon them, and they spoke with tongues and prophesied."*

When Jesus ascended and was seated at the right hand of God in heaven, He sent the Holy Spirit to possess and control the lives of His followers, taking His own place of leadership in their lives. The *filling of the Spirit* is an added dimension to the indwelling Spirit. This can happen immediately (when we first come to Jesus), but like Apollos, often takes further teaching accompanied by a deliberate surrender to and receiving of the Spirit.

The *filling of the Holy Spirit* is not a one-time event. The verb tense of Paul's command in Ephesians 5:18 reveals this, emphatically declaring, *"Be being filled with the Holy Spirit!"* We are consistently being filled as we submit to the Spirit's ways, aligning and fellowshipping with Him in an ongoing manner. We regularly evaluate our hearts, confessing areas where we have grieved and failed to rely on Him. Laying these down, we realign to receive His filling. We don't allow emotions or our five senses to determine whether we are "filled" or not. Instead, by faith, we stand on God's Word as being true.

For more details about the "Spirit-filled Life," see the author's book *Engaging the Holy Spirit: Understanding His Dynamics Among Believers Toward the Fulfillment of the Great Commission* (IGNITE Media, 2012).

I. Walking in the Spirit (Romans 8:1-5)

In the first five verses in Romans 8, Paul puts significant focus on two life perspectives with three statements about _"those who do not walk according to the flesh, but according to the Spirit"_ (vs. 1, 4, 5). Verse 5 helps us understand _how_ to walk in the Spirit. _"Those who live according to the flesh set their minds on the things of the flesh, but those who live according to the Spirit, the things of the Spirit."_

We see a contrast in this verse surrounding the core issue of our mindsets. Where a believer chooses to put their mindset directly impacts whether they walk according to the flesh or Spirit. _"Setting our minds on things of the flesh"_ means allowing mindsets to dominate our thinking that originate (1) from what our five senses can tangibly experience, (2) what our emotions tell us at any given moment, (3) what our physical appetites or impulses may dictate, or (4) what our circumstances and situations are like.

In contrast, living according to the Spirit refers to finding out what the Bible and the Spirit say about our lives and circumstances and applying these truths. These then begin to dominate the conversation within ourselves and with God instead of what we are experiencing in the natural world. This is the essence of the life of faith.

It is common to find believers living for years, even decades, with a dominant mindset determined by what they can see, feel, hear or emotions being experienced at a particular time. They face difficult circumstances and easily cave because their life perspective is not on God's truth but on the overwhelming nature of their circumstance or what their emotions are telling them.

J. Inheriting Spiritual Power – The Signs of the Kingdom (Acts 1:8)

Acts 1:8 provides a promise to every born-again believer. Jesus relates, _"But you shall receive power when the Holy Spirit has come upon_ *you; and you shall be witnesses to Me in Jerusalem, and in all Judea and Samaria, and to the end of the earth."* The word *power* implies strength based on inherent physical, spiritual or natural powers. Believers would now have the Holy Spirit *indwelling* them, and as they allowed, He would *fill* them, based on Jesus' delegated authority (Matthew 28:18). This *power* has a clear purpose noted in the text – *to be His witnesses.* Spiritual power is never meant to merely "wow" people but reveal Jesus as King and supreme authority over all created order, submitting to His Lordship.

We have seen that Jesus' first coming was for the purpose of inaugurating the Kingdom. We also know a purpose of the Holy Spirit's coming at Pentecost (Acts 2:1-4) was to continue the spread of that Kingdom in this age throughout the world. What then are visible, biblical signs the hidden Kingdom of God is being expressed among a people? These signs reveal to all ethnic peoples the initial age of the Kingdom is upon us.

Scripture reveals at least 17 specific items, signs of the Kingdom, though this list is evidently not exhaustive. All these are not necessarily happening at the same time but over time reveal the Kingdom of God is being experienced among a people. We find the first six signs in Isaiah 61 – (1) Preaching the Gospel to the poor (2) Healing the brokenhearted (3) Preaching deliverance to the captives (4) Restoring sight to the blind (5) Liberating the oppressed (6) Instituting the acceptable year of the Lord. Where these are happening the Kingdom of God has come upon a people.

Another six were seen throughout Jesus' own life and ministry. Scripture reveals these continue and increase among those taking Jesus at His word (John 14:12). The global Church is continuing "to do and teach" (Acts 1:1) what Jesus did among all people groups. (7) Healing the sick (8) Casting out evil spirits (9) Making lame people walk (10) Cleansing lepers (11) Restoring hearing to the deaf (12) Raising the dead.[xxxix]

The book of Acts, in many places, reveals *"signs and wonders"* taking place through the people of God (Acts 2:43; Acts 5:12; Acts 6:8; Acts 14:3). However, we are not told exactly what these are. There is a differentiation in the text related to physical healing and deliverance and *"signs and wonders."* It appears Luke was describing something other than healings and deliverances when highlighting *"signs and wonders."* Thus another sign of the Kingdom would be (13) Signs and wonders (miracles) of varying sorts.

The purpose of spiritual power highlighted in Acts 1:8 reveals its primary purpose, *"...to be My witnesses in Judea, Samaria and the ends of the earth."* Thus, a sign of the Kingdom among a people is their (14) Deliberate scattering to near-culture ethnic peoples with the Gospel of the Kingdom. Three further signs of the Kingdom include a (15) Deep, convicting work of the Holy Spirit that Jesus is Lord and King (John 16:8) and the (16) Sharing of material goods (Acts 2:45; 4:34) with one another and (17) The operations of the gifts of the Holy Spirit in their midst.

K. Living Holy, Blameless and Victorious Lives (Psalm 101:2)

The Holy Spirit indwells believers to release the life of Jesus into our hearts. Soon after becoming born again, we become conscious of the inner battle raging – the clash between human nature and spirit. Paul revealed in Galatians 5:17, *"For the flesh lusts against the Spirit, and the Spirit against the flesh, and these are contrary to one another, so that you do not do the things that you wish."* Left to ourselves, the flesh (human nature) frequently wins, so many believers have given up the fight and are content to live with a measure of the flesh dominating their lives. Human beings, in our own strength, cannot defeat the power and temptations of sin. Yet, the Holy Spirit in us can. As we submit to Him, He releases power to overcome.

Peter teaches in 1 Peter 2:11, *"Beloved, I beg you as sojourners and pilgrims, abstain from fleshly lusts which war against the soul."* There are a variety of "fleshly lusts" referred to here, but a strong emphasis is related to sexual immorality. The Bible regularly cautions of this serious area of bondage and how easily it enslaves the people of God. In opposition to this area of the flesh, Paul reveals in Galatians 5:24-25, *"And those who are Christ's have crucified the flesh with its passions and desires. If we live in the Spirit, let us also walk in the Spirit."*

We are identified spiritually with Christ in His crucifixion as Paul clarifies in Galatians 2:20-21: *"I have been crucified with Christ ; it is no longer I who live, but Christ lives in me; and the life which I now live in the flesh I live by faith in the Son of God, who loved me and gave Himself for me."* As a result, *"The body of sin has been done away with, that we should no longer be slaves to sin"* (Romans 6:6).

This is what is happening in Romans 7-8 as Paul relates his own struggles with the flesh. Chapter 7 focuses on his anguish and failure, and chapter 8 introduces the Holy Spirit who empowers him, delivering him from the power of sin. In Romans 8:37, Paul can honestly declare, *"For in all things we are more than conquerors through Him who loved us."*

Believers should have no addictions. We ought to be free from spiritual oppression and emotional depression, overcoming every temptation coming our way. Paul again clarifies this truth plainly for us in Romans 6:17-18, *"But God be thanked that though you were slaves of sin, yet you obeyed from the heart that form of doctrine to which you were delivered. And having been set free from sin, you became slaves of righteousness."*

L. Growing in God's Word – The Bible (Psalm 119:9-16)

Born-again believers embrace the Bible as God's perfect revelation to all humanity, written by the Holy Spirit through the medium of human beings under His leadership and sway. Everything contained in it is absolute truth. Believers give themselves to growing in experiential knowledge of the Bible throughout their lifetimes.

We can now understand the Word in increasing ways because the Holy Spirit indwells us. The Bible is meant to be taken at face value, acted upon, its truths implemented into our lives. Every believer applies themselves by reading, studying and praying the Bible, asking the Spirit to release spiritual understanding through it. The truths of Scripture are not merely memorized but applied to everyday life circumstances, made real as believers prove their reality. It is God's will that all believers embrace a lifestyle as a vibrant student of God's word, applying all that is gleaned, making truth real in their own lives. This is not merely for pastors and Christian leaders but every born-again believer.

Feeding, meditating and praying God's word is not merely a good idea. It is the primary way the Holy Spirit releases spiritual strength among believers to stand for God and His Kingdom. Believers neglecting the privilege of going deep with God through His word are forgoing a key way for God's people to live in victory. Rooting ourselves in God's word empowers us to be vigilant against temptation while discerning His voice and walking according to His will.

A necessary development in the life of every believer is a *Bible Study Action Plan*. This is a personal plan to help daily grow as a student of God's word. There are two portions of such a plan. First is a daily devotional plan, and second is a book-by-book plan for in-depth study.

Make a plan to devotionally read two Psalms, a Proverb and a chapter in the Gospels daily. As you read, commit to "prayer-reading." Don't merely read the words but interact with God using the truths line by line in the verses. Ask yourself and the Holy Spirit questions about the text: (1) What are promises to be received in this verse? (2) What are actions to do in this verse? (3) What does it teach me about God? (4) About myself and others? (5) How can I align with God's will related to this verse? By praying the truths of the Bible, our spiritual lives grow as we experience God and His Word in a growing dimension.

Additionally, we undertake in-depth study of the Bible. Every believer is meant to be a lifelong student of God's Word. Invite the Spirit to lead you to particular Bible books each year to study in depth. Write a list of the Bible books. To do in-depth study, it is helpful to find two or more reputable commentaries or book studies about the Bible book (these can be found free online) and get a journal to take notes in. The first step is to read the Bible book "as a whole." Try to read through the book quickly, in one sitting if possible. You will see things in a one-time reading that you would not see when you break it up. Identify the big picture purpose of the book, its context, place in biblical history and general teaching. Second, go back to the beginning of the book and begin to take a passage at a time (maybe 4-10 verses), read it, and invite the Spirit to speak about the meaning and purpose of the text. Then, take notes concerning the insights you see about the text and what spiritual revelation God provides to grasp His ways and will.

M. Growing in Communion Prayer (Joshua 1:5-8)

Born-again believers possess constant access to the throne of God in prayer. The wall of separation from God in prayer has been torn away because of Jesus' own righteousness. God has created us to enjoy a personal, thriving, growing prayer life with Him. Prayer has often been reduced to merely seeking God for things, for help in times of need. There is obviously a place for this, yet prayer is much more. Prayer is the reflection of our relationship with God. Our prayer lives reveal what type of relationship we enjoy with Him. Is it near, intimate, vibrant – or casual, distant, lifeless? It entirely depends on our willingness to pursue a consistent and growing prayer life with God. He is always there waiting for us to engage.

There are at least two kinds of prayer believers are growing in: communion and intercessory prayer. Communion prayer focuses on God for who He is. We talk to Him about our desire to grow in Him and to have our hearts expanded. We ask Him to reveal more of Himself to us, showing us His glory, beauty, and ways, fascinating and causing us to awe at who He is and what He is like. When we see more of Him, our hearts respond with deeper love and devotion to Him. We meditate on His attributes, characteristics, work and ways, responding with adoration and worship.

Communion prayer takes deliberate effort and sacrifice to maintain. There is a cost. We need a measure of abandonment to walk in it. We choose to put away distractions, setting ourselves upon Him. Many things arise to keep believers from growing in intimate fellowship with God. Pressures, needs, deadlines, friends, etc., come to the forefront when we commit to going deep with God in communion prayer.

N. Growing in Intercessory Prayer (Matthew 5:9-13)

Intercessory prayer is Jesus' chosen way to release heaven's resources on the earth. It's God's primary means of moving His eternal plans and purposes forward. Intercessory prayer is prayer on behalf of people, families, cities, nations and situations. We stand in their place, contending for the will of God, transformation, conviction of sin and the influence of the Kingdom among them. There is a law in the Kingdom of God that this type of intercession, committed to faithfully, produces results. We don't know how long it may take, but if we stick with it, aligning with God's conditions of intercession, He will not fail to act.

It's easy to misunderstand prayer. Many believers think if we bother God long enough, He will answer. We get into crisis situations and pray with zeal for the circumstance to get righted. Our prayer is shrouded in worry, anxiety and turmoil. However, effective prayer emerges from a grateful heart at peace and quiet before God, even though we might be in a swirl of challenging and emotional circumstances. Prayer requires a heart waiting on the Lord in the place of rest. Learning to live perpetually before Him in stillness is needed to operate according to God's ways of prayer and intercession. This contrasts with the inner upheaval, worry and turmoil often experienced in our prayer lives.

Prayer, in its simplest form, is a cycle. Through the Spirit, we discover what God wants in a given situation, and we intercede for His revealed will to be accomplished. We pray what is on His heart and, in response, God works according to His perfect will. God could take our little piece out of the prayer cycle and be just fine. But because of His eternal plan to partner with His people in bringing His Kingdom, He involves our small efforts and uses them for His glory.

O. Hearing His Voice (John 10:1-5)

In order to hear the voice of God, we have to learn the ways God speaks. The Lord loves us, wanting to speak, but because we don't know what His voice sounds like we often miss it. It is one of the most significant privileges of the Kingdom of God that the King lowers Himself to talk about His Kingdom plans with us.

The God of the universe wants to speak to us, but we can't enter the dialogue unless we are able to hear and understand what He is saying. The real problem is we have not cultivated what some have called the "hearing ear." The hearing ear distinguishes the voice of God in the midst of many competing voices in our daily lives (John10:27). Most of these fall into one of three categories: the voice of others (the world), our own imaginations (the flesh), or a thought that has been planted by the enemy (the devil).

I learned a practice early in my walk with God. When I think I might have heard His voice, I take authority in Jesus' name over the voices of others, my imagination, and the enemy, silencing them and asking God to clarify whether or not it is Him who is speaking. With these other voices silenced through His authority, the thought, impression, or inner voice will either strengthen - confirming it is from Him - or disappear, proving it to be one of the competing voices.

Growing in discerning God's voice takes practice. We begin by waiting patiently in prayer, listening to what we hear, and then write it down in a journal. Then, take what was heard and test it against the Bible. Often, God will speak to His children through the Bible. As we read the Word of God, we have certain words jump off the page, seemingly more important than the other words. This is the Holy Spirit speaking. Pray over that word or phrase and ask God what He wants to say about it. He will give pictures and impressions about what to do based upon those scriptures. Even if the Lord does not give a specific Scripture, His words will resonate as aligning with Scripture.

This practice demands a discipline: listening and waiting. We cannot expect Him to speak if He knows we are not actively listening. Would you speak to someone who wasn't showing you they cared about listening to you? Will we put in the time and energy to wait and actively listen for His voice in the secret place?

God speaks in many different ways. He desires us to hear His voice as we read the Word of God, highlighting certain Scriptures and speaking about how those Scriptures apply to our lives. He wants the words He speaks to affect the way we live. The Lord can speak through dreams and visions as we see in the lives of Joseph in Genesis 37:5-9, Peter in Acts 10:9-16, or Paul in Acts 16:9-10. The Lord can also speak through angelic visitations, such as with Cornelius in Acts 10:31-32 or Mary in Luke 1:28. As we are praying, the Lord will give you a Scripture that becomes a powerful weapon to bring freedom, deliverance, or answer to prayer.

God can also speak through many other forms. He can speak through movies, books, or other forms of print or electronic media. The Lord can talk to us through other people or His creation all around us. The God of the universe is not limited in how He can speak. He is only limited by what we are able to hear. Are we listening? Are we tuned in and ready for Him to speak?

It is good to keep a journal of the ways God speaks. By writing it down, it will be easier to identify patterns in the way God speaks and make it easier to discern His voice. After seeing different patterns, it is always good to ask God to open up new ways of speaking. If there is a particular way of hearing God's voice that seems interesting, ask God to speak in that way and then wait and expect God to speak. I have journals filled with over 20 years of specific things God has spoken to me about life and ministry in many different ways.

P. Engaging Jesus' Spiritual Authority (Matthew 28:18)

Born-again believers possess spiritual authority to stand against every attack, plan, assignment and scheme of Satan over our lives, circumstances, finances, relationships, property, families, workplaces, towns, cities and nations. In Matthew 28:18, Jesus declares a startling truth. This teaching comes following His crucifixion and resurrection from the dead. He has accomplished the work necessary to restore the lost Kingdom of God, opening the way for all peoples to experience life as He intended it for all time. He states victoriously, *"All authority has been given to me in heaven and on earth."* The implication is that He now joyfully delegates that authority to born-again believers as we go about the work of the Kingdom of God.

We are not helpless before Satan's attacks. We have been given Jesus' authority to stand against his fiery attacks. Paul elaborates on our battle against the kingdom of darkness in Ephesians 6:10-11: *"Finally, my brethren, be strong in the Lord and in the power of His might. Put on the whole armor of God, that you may be able to stand against the wiles of the devil."* Through the death and resurrection of Jesus, believers possess power with God, resisting the evil one over every area. When we discern spiritual forces of darkness are interfering in our midst, we take a stand in Jesus, rebuking and resisting their power in His superior authority.

Q. Experiencing Healing and Deliverance (Psalm 103:1-5)

New life in the Kingdom includes available deliverance related to our body, soul, mind and spirit from all addictions and spiritual bondages. It is not God's will for unhealthy habits to dominate us. Many believers have given up the fight against the flesh, content to be a believer addicted to a variety of issues contrary to the will of God. There is deliverance and freedom available from all these as we take Him at His word.

Jesus' inheritance includes experiencing healing of emotional, physical, psychological, relational and spiritual wounds, restoring soundness in every area. It is not His will for sickness and disease to dominate the people of God. In addition Jesus Himself had told the disciples they could expect to do greater works then even He did (John 14:12), because they would receive the same Holy Spirit which operated within Him.

Jesus has given us spiritual power through the outpouring of His Spirit at Pentecost. This authority is what all healing is based on. Invoking Jesus' name in prayer is a declaration of spiritual authority to heal.[xl] We want to regularly and continually pray for the full range of healing from the Lord to restore wholeness. Sometimes, such restoration is immediate, while at other times it unfolds seemingly unnoticed over a period of time. We pray in this way among those in the Kingdom as well as without. We use Jesus' Kingdom authority in healing and deliverance among the peoples of the world. Many are drawn into the Kingdom of God through seeing or personally experiencing such healing and deliverance. These were two important aspects of Jesus' own ministry that modern disciples are meant to walk in as well.

R. Growing in Supernatural Love (Ephesians 3:16-19)

Being a born-again believer means we have a new heart in which the primary characteristic is love. The Holy Spirit, indwelling believers when we were born again, roots us in Christ, meaning we are rooted and grounded in love (Ephesians 3:17; Colossians 2:7). We have the capacity to grow in receiving love from God and loving Him back, while simultaneously growing in love for one another. Paul reveals in many places that love is the centerpiece of the new life of a believer (Romans 13:9; 1 Corinthians 13; Ephesians 5:2).

Jesus taught the greatest commandment (in Matthew 22:37) is _"You shall love the Lord your God with all your heart, with all your soul, and with all your mind."_ The hallmark of faith in Jesus is a thriving and growing, give-and-take love relationship with Jesus Christ, who is fully God. 1 John 4:19 reveals, _"We love Him because He first loved us!"_ Our love for Him is a response of His love first for us. This means it is necessary to be consistently growing in our capacity to be receiving love from Him. We want to grow in these two dynamics (receiving and giving love from and to Him) throughout our lives, giving ourselves over and over to growing in this supernatural love. Simultaneously, we want to help others walk in this same measure of receiving and giving supernatural love in growing dimensions.

S. God's Powerful Presence (Deuteronomy 31:1-8)

No longer alone, His abiding presence never leaves or forsakes us. Throughout the Bible, we find God making one promise over and over to His people. _"Do not fear...I am with you!"_ What a glorious fact. Though His presence is always with us, the measure we experience it is reliant upon how deep we are willing to go with God in fellowship and intimacy. We want to experience His presence in our daily lives by cultivating His presence, sensing His nearness, seeing His orchestrating hand at work. His powerful presence provides confidence to face and overcome difficult situations.

We walk with God, finding Him a present help in time of need. We prove His goodness by seeing His promises in Scripture brought into experience. We unlock God's mysteries using the key of faith and open God's vast treasure chest by the means of prayer. We experience God as our defender, strong tower, mighty fortress, a very present help, the One who intervenes in our circumstances. He orchestrates details to accomplish His will in and through our lives and undertakes to bring forth His purposes among those submitted to Him. When we go through challenges, we look to the tangible presence of God in the above ways. This doesn't necessarily happen every day, nor do we feel victorious all the time. But the overall bent of our lives is in this direction. None of this is based on earning or deserving Kingdom benefits but on His mercy alone, lavishing us with that which is undeserved.

T. Experiencing Favor and Blessed Circumstances (Psalm 5:12)

God desires His people to experience His favor and blessing within their lives. The Kingdom of God releases the very blessings of the age to come to God's people, making them available to those walking according to His ways. These Kingdom blessings are available and are to be applied to every area of our lives. This does not mean all will go well consistently. We are not to measure our lives in God by whether or not we are consistently experiencing good or difficult situations. Yet we are to see that God wants to shower a richness of spiritual and natural blessings upon His people. These blessings are already ours before God yet are received (or applied) by faith into our situations, persevering over time in seeing them released in our midst. Psalm 5:12 says, *"For You, O Lord, will bless the righteous; With favor You will surround him as with a shield."* There is favor available in all situations of life. We contend in the Spirit for all the promises God has given to us. We don't know the timeframes but commit to believe and rid our hearts of the nagging temptation to doubt God.

Summary of Phase Three

Many believers are not living according to these blessings provided as our free and always available inheritance. They are saved, yet they choose to live in spiritual poverty, not according to the glorious benefits freely supplied and meant for our full partaking in the Kingdom of God in this age. To grow as mature followers of Jesus it is incumbent upon us to gratefully receive all He has lavishly and graciously provided. Apart from doing so it is very difficult to effectively engage with *Phase Four.* Let's continue to press on to the fullness of all God has for us in *Phase Four.*

7

PHASE FOUR

The Responsibilities of the Kingdom

It is common for believers to understand their salvation as primarily what happens when they die. Though we are indescribably grateful for the truth of eternal fellowship with God, there is so much more we are meant to cooperate with in the Kingdom of God throughout this life. Believers develop as true disciples in *Phase Three*, laying hold of the vast inheritance of the Kingdom of God available to them. Yet, this is where even more stop. Some disciples take all the benefits and blessings but shy away from the responsibility of living according to God's ways, conforming to Jesus' Kingdom purpose in this age. They want the good stuff, but when God's Kingdom purposes encroach on their lives, they push back. These have failed to embrace their core Kingdom calling as Jesus' bondservants, surrendered to His will.

Phase Four of the Gospel of the Kingdom – Citizens of the Kingdom Are Responsible to Live According to Its Ways and Principles, Spreading It Among All Ethnic Peoples Globally

Many believers misunderstand the biblical meaning of the "free gift of salvation," overlooking the meaning of "free." We do not earn God's righteousness nor restored relationship with Him. It is "free" because of Jesus' love revealed through the cross and resurrection. For those embracing this free gift, there are expectations and responsibilities before God. It is not "free" in the sense of living however we choose. It is "freedom" to live according to God's created, intended order, His will. If we rightly receive His "free gift of salvation," the only adequate response is gratefully, joyfully giving ourselves to His expectations.

The Gospel of the Kingdom empowers all peoples to embrace these responsibilities with deep joy, obedience and faithfulness, serving His Kingdom purposes.

Embracing Responsibilities

Phase Four focuses on responsibilities as citizens of the Kingdom of God. It answers the question of how being sons and daughters of the Kingdom influences daily living related to the Kingdom of God being realized in the world. This is the human response to the divine blessings, benefits and privileges of *Phase Three*. In response to the lavish and extraordinary goodness of God believers align our will, ways, plans and purposes with God's, making our lives no longer about our desires and goals, but supremely fixed on His. As peoples from all ethnic groups come to saving faith in Jesus, they are taught how to cooperate with the vast inheritance provided them, living according to Jesus' Kingdom standards.

A necessary starting point of *Phase Four* is asking believers the following question, determining the life perspective we take on our faith. How every born-again believer answers this simple question reveals much about their ability to engage rightly in the responsibilities of *Phase Four*. *Does God mainly exist for me (my comfort, well-being, possessions, convenience) or do I primarily exist for God (to love, worship, please and magnify Him, bringing Him great glory and honor)*? Of course, it's true, as we've seen in *Phase Three*, God provides a rich inheritance of benefits, blessings and privileges. Yet if our overall faith perspective is fixed on "me" it is tainted by self and not what God intended. While taking the perspective that my life is meant to please Him, as a grateful response to His eternal love, and bring Him glory in the earth prepares me to respond to His calling, even when doing so includes sacrifice.

One reason Jesus' Great Commission (Matthew 28:18-20) is taking so long is a lack of the body of Christ taking *Phase Four* seriously. While the second coming of Christ is the next great date on the timeline of redemptive history, God has bound Himself so that event will not take place apart from the fulfilling of the Great Commission first. Fulfilling the Great Commission is Jesus' Kingdom priority in this age.

Some are not taught this phase, while others rationalize it away. Instead, we must embrace *Phase Four* in proclaiming the Kingdom among all peoples. We teach these truths in context of helping believers grow in maturity. Some might be new believers, while others might have been believers for awhile. With both, we invite them to understand the body of Christ's responsibilities, becoming personally engaged in them.

The Keys of the Kingdom

Jesus tells Peter in Matthew 16:18-19, *"And on this rock I will build My church, and the gates of Hades shall not prevail against it. <u>And I will give you the keys of the kingdom of heaven,</u> and whatever you bind on earth will be bound in heaven, and whatever you loose on earth will be loosed in heaven."* Though Peter is a representative, the promise of the "keys of the Kingdom" is to all Kingdom believers. Creator God, having provided the initial way of restoration of the lost Kingdom through the death and resurrection of Jesus, now gives His people keys to build His Church globally among all peoples and sub-cultures. Every born-again believer has been given keys of the Kingdom, not merely pastors and Christian leaders, but all who experience new life in His Kingdom.

Let's consider some of the following areas of responsibility we are meant to be embracing in His Kingdom.

A. Living Wholeheartedly for God (Philippians 3:8-10)

Those acknowledging Jesus as King commit themselves to wholehearted faith. Jesus has revealed no other alternative in His

Kingdom than wholehearted commitment to Himself. Half-hearted or casual faith is not a biblical idea. Jesus revealed in Matthew 22:37, *"You shall love the Lord your God* with all your heart, mind, soul and strength..."* The righteous God invites Kingdom citizens, enjoying covenantal relationship, to live wholeheartedly according to His ways and righteousness.

There is no greater way to live. The human heart was meant to experience delighting ourselves in God and being delighted by the beautiful God. We receive the blessings, benefits and privileges of the new birth. We guard our hearts against the temptation to slumber in grace, instead moving upward and onward in Jesus all the days of our lives.

When love for God grows, capacity to surrender all for the object of affection also grows. We abandon all in exchange for Him – submitting to His leadership in our lives and ministries. A human life becoming more possessed by the Holy Spirit is the greatest gift of God to the world. We reflect His values, align with what He supremely regards, receive His renewing power, and partner in the big picture purposes of His Kingdom in this age and the age to come. To accomplish this, we grow in wholehearted love for Jesus throughout our lifetime.

B. Embracing the 'Sermon on the Mount' Lifestyle (Matthew 5-7)

The Sermon on the Mount is one of Jesus' most important teachings. He reveals how believers, interacting with the Kingdom of God, are meant to practically live. The primary point is believers become true disciples by cultivating eight beatitudes with focus and wholeheartedness (5:3-12) – *becoming poor in spirit, mourning, being meek, hungering and thirsting for righteousness, being merciful, being pure in heart, being peacemakers, and willingly embracing persecution for the right reasons.* Through growing in the beatitudes, disciples impact the nations as salt, light and a city on a hill (5:13-16), producing a global harvest for the Kingdom. Fulfilling the Great Commission is millions of believers cultivating the eight beatitudes in their individual lives, operating as "salt" and "light" among their communities. They declare and live out the gospel of Christ and His Kingdom among all peoples globally.

The Sermon on the Mount continues by revealing how this growing harvest of people enthroning Jesus as Lord live according to a different standard of life - *the Kingdom of God.* This happens first by growing in righteousness in six areas common to all humanity (5:17-48) and then faithfully embracing seven Kingdom activities (6:1 - 7:21).

The six areas Jesus highlights to grow in righteousness are: (1) Resisting anger; (2) Overcoming sin; (3) Honoring marriage; (4) Keeping our word; (5) Refusing retaliation and defensiveness; and (6) Loving our enemies.

The seven Kingdom activities to engage in include: (1) Giving correctly; (2) praying correctly; (3) fasting correctly; (4) pursuing true treasure; (5) overcoming worry and anxiety; (6) a disciple and their relationships; and (7) a disciple guarding their ways. These seven activities relate to disciples living in submission to Jesus. It is important that disciples become committed students of the Sermon on the Mount, embracing and obeying it.

For an in-depth study on the Sermon on the Mount see the author's *Studies in the Sermon on the Mount: A Call To Kingdom Life as True Disciples* (IGNITE Media, 2016)

C. Putting on the 'New Man' (Romans 13:11-14)

As born-again believers, experiencing the benefits, blessings and privileges of the Kingdom of God, we *put off* our old conduct while *putting on* new habits, attitudes, and the "new man" God has provided us. Paul teaches this crucial concept beginning in Ephesians 4:17. *"You should no longer walk as the Gentiles walk, in the futility of their mind, having their understanding darkened, being alienated from the life of God."* He clarifies believers are now different from the rest of the world.

Peoples of the world are dominated by the evil influences therein, not having their spirit made alive in Christ. Though we are in the world, we have been changed and are now not of it. We no longer allow our minds to dwell on things we used to, instead we *"set our minds on things above, not on things on the earth* (Colossians 3:2)." Through Christ, we are *"renewed in the spirit of our mind"* (Ephesians 4:23).

The spiritual understanding of the people of the world is darkened. The light of God's truth, beauty and power has not yet penetrated their experience. They are alienated from the life of God, separated, cut off, without knowing it. People of the world *"have given themselves over to lewdness, to work all uncleanness with greediness"* (Ephesians 4:19), while born-again believers *"put off concerning your former conduct, the old man, which grows corrupt according to the deceitful lusts, and be renewed in the spirit of your mind, and that you put on the new man which was created according to God, in true righteousness and holiness"* (Ephesians 4:22).

D. Cultivating the 'Abiding Lifestyle' (John 15:4)

Disciples cultivate the abiding lifestyle intended by the Father, learning to sit at Jesus' feet. Jesus provides a vivid example in Luke 10:39: *"And she had a sister called Mary, who also sat at Jesus' feet and heard His word."* Believers learn to sit at His feet, drinking of Him, waiting in His presence, walking in the Spirit in love and active obedience. Abiding does not happen overnight. It takes much time in His presence, talking to Him, listening to Him, discerning truth in His word. This is obviously a privilege (Phase Three) yet also a responsibility in His Kingdom as our hearts are softened, sensitized, filled up with God by abiding in Him.

In John 15:5, Jesus reveals, *"I am the vine, you are the branches. He who abides in Me and I in Him, bears much fruit; for without Me you can do nothing."* He is revealing a crucial principle. God is the source of all supernatural life (vine). Human beings, rightly related to God, are the conduits of His supernatural life on earth (branches). We are meant to produce great Kingdom fruit (both internal and external). The only means by which this is possible is abiding in Christ. Abiding, Jesus reveals, binds us (branches) together with the source of true life and power (vine).

E. Seek First the Kingdom of God (Matthew 6:33)

Citizens of the Kingdom prioritize the Kingdom. The people of God throughout history have tended to neglect His core purposes while being preoccupied with personal concerns. When this happens, God intervenes, seeking to wake us up to prioritize what He cares about supremely.

Human beings naturally worry about having material needs met. Jesus taught a key strategy to keep disciples from getting caught up with worry and anxiety. *"But seek first the Kingdom of God and His righteousness and all these things shall be added unto you"* (Matthew 6:33). Prioritizing the Kingdom is a call to grow in faith by aligning our priorities with God's.

Possessing growing vision of the Kingdom of God established on earth makes it more difficult to be sidetracked by worry over material needs. Seeking first the Kingdom and His righteousness is two-fold: growing in daily experiential knowledge of Jesus and developing a burden for His will in the earth, being activated in these purposes.

By contrast, when spiritual life is dull, with little of the abiding presence and blessing of God, the reason might be wrong priorities. This usually includes self-centered preoccupations with family, personal and material concerns instead of Kingdom-centered zeal and purpose. The biblical pattern of reestablishing an abiding sense of the presence of God is making the Kingdom the priority it is meant to be in the life of every disciple.

F. Holding Fast Our Confidence (Hebrews 3:6)

Kingdom citizens are diligent in the daily life of faith, maintaining intimacy with Jesus, guarding from the natural tendency to plateau and spiritually taper off that allows a cold heart toward God to set in. They remain sensitive to the Lord, moving forward in faith instead of losing spiritual ground and backsliding.

Hebrews 3:6 communicates an often overlooked truth, *"Whose house we are if we hold fast the confidence and the rejoicing of the hope firm to the end."* And just a few verses later, the writer confirms this again in 3:14: *"For we have become partakers of Christ if we hold fast the beginning of our confidence steadfast until the end."* In both verses, there is the conditional word "if." If believers hold fast to confidence to the end, the passage indicates, we will be saved.

The reverse then is the implication of the text. That beginning the life of faith in Jesus, receiving the new birth, partaking of some of the benefits of the Kingdom, doesn't mean all will "hold fast" their confidence (heart belief in God) to the end. The "end" is that of each person's life journey. We are meant to continuously stoke our hearts onward and upward in Christ, actively "believing" throughout our lifetimes. This heart-level belief is reflected in every aspect of our lives.

Paul adds a final verse confirming this idea in Colossians 1:23: *"To present you holy and blameless...if indeed you continue in the faith, grounded and steadfast, and are not moved away from the hope of the gospel you have heard... ."* The context clarifies Paul is referring to remaining steady in the application of heartfelt belief in Christ if we expect to be reconciled to God in the future Kingdom of God.

It is clear from an honest, Holy Spirit-illuminated look at the New Testament that believers can lose their future in the Kingdom of God if their faith is neglected and sidelined. We are not talking about stumbling in sin or having a few bad weeks or months – but ongoing, willful rebellion, no longer valuing the inheritance given them through Christ. They began well but didn't remain steadfast, failing to implement habits necessary to endure through the ups and downs of life. They fell away, failing to pay attention to the multitude of ways the Spirit convicted, rebuked, corrected and disciplined, wooing them back to the Lord. God works overtime to bring back the backslider, and some return with wholeheartedness. Yet, many refuse His invitations, continuing a downward spiral of destruction. The New Testament is full of teaching about them. They are part of the great apostasy, those failing to continue in the faith, failing to be confident until the end (Matthew 24:12; 1 Thessalonians 2:3; 1 Timothy 4:1).

It is common for believers to become disappointed, disillusioned, a low-grade anger toward God setting in over time. They buy into a false narrative of the life of faith. When life doesn't go how they think it should, a sense of being ripped off settles in. If this offense at God isn't addressed and confessed, aligning once again with God's ways, we easily slip into a backslidden state.

G. Living Crucified and Resurrected Lives (Galatians 2:20)

The crucified life refers to denying ourselves, taking up our cross, following Jesus. Paul said in Galatians 6:14, *"I boast in the cross."* He had a two-fold idea in mind. First, he "boasted" in the redemptive work Jesus obediently endured on the cross. Secondly, through the cross, supernatural power is available for all peoples to be restored to right relationship with God and His eternal Kingdom.

Jesus' cross was the foundation, yet boasting in the cross included believers' following Jesus' example by taking up their own crosses, denying themselves. Spiritual power is released through a life embracing Christ's work on the cross, following His footsteps by denying themselves, and embracing their own crosses. Practically, this means whenever our will clashes with the will of God, we submit plans, ambitions and desires unto Him. Through these two sides of Paul's writings, spiritual power and Kingdom transformation are experienced. Resurrection life refers to the power of Christ's overcoming life activated in life in every area. His victories are ours, and everything available through His resurrection authority is now available to us as we lay hold of it in each fresh situation.

H. Walking Worthy of the Gospel (Colossians 1:10)

Believers are responsible to walk according to the ways of God and His Kingdom. We obey the teachings of the New Testament related to walking in holiness, denying our flesh, living for God's glory on the earth. We honor Him with finances and material possessions, overcoming greed and covetousness. This is primarily done through faithfulness with money, tithes and offerings. Faithfulness in finances is not merely about money but allegiance to God in our lives. As we obediently handle finances, He reveals Himself as the great provider and source of all physical sustenance. He gives creative ideas and holy strategies to supply for needs while also having enough to sow into His global harvest.

We honor Him with our bodies, living obediently to His standards of sexuality – freeing us to enjoy sexuality to its fullest capacity in the confines of marriage between one man and one woman, yet resisting it outside of this boundary. This is one of the greatest areas of temptation today. The enemy has unleashed a strategic onslaught of sexual immorality against the body of Christ globally, and he is not letting up. Believers must learn to stand against his attacks in this area, learning to resist and refuse the powerful lure of sexual temptation through the Holy Spirit.

I. Becoming A Witness (Acts 1:8)

Every born-again believer is called as a witness. A witness is someone who speaks from firsthand experience, describing something they've seen. The first apostles in the book of Acts revealed a Person they had lived with for three years, events they had seen with their own physical eyes. How can we, who live 2,000 plus years after the life of Jesus, bear such a witness?

First, through experiencing Jesus in and through Scripture. We see Him teaching truth everywhere He goes; watch Him heal and forgive; loving everybody, even the outcasts; we see Him arrested, tried and crucified; watch Him break all natural barriers and rise from the dead. Second, Jesus comes to us through the Word of God, by the Holy Spirit. Through seeing and believing in this One we experience in the Bible we are led into our own death and resurrection. Dying to ourselves, desires, rights, plans, purposes and sinful nature itself and being resurrected with a brand new life on the inside. We now experience Jesus' power active within our lives. He is no longer simply a unique Person in history. He is present in our day to day lives. Our witness is not looking back to Jesus in history but proclaiming a King alive and active today.

As a result of experiencing Jesus firsthand we reveal to others what we have seen - a Person we have experienced as reality in our own lives. We proclaim the life-changing, history-shaping significance of this Person and the works of His life, death, resurrection, ascension, outpouring of the Spirit and the culmination of history in Himself in His second coming. We don't need to be trained theologians and professional preachers. The Kingdom has advanced most effectively when ordinary believers, experiencing the living Christ in their daily lives, have shared Him spontaneously and naturally with those around them.[xli] This happens in the marketplace, on the job with coworkers, in the gym, on the public transport and in many other natural circumstances. We use our daily situations as opportunities to naturally discuss what we have experienced with those around us.

J. Embracing Jesus' Commission As Our Own (Matthew 28:18-20)

These truths bring us to a culminating fact: All believers bear responsibility for the Great Commission, proclaiming and demonstrating good news related to the God of Creation, His redeeming work for all, His Kingdom now and yet to come. The global body of Jesus Christ, empowered by the Holy Spirit, is meant to proclaim and demonstrate the Gospel of the Kingdom across all barriers to every ethnic people group on earth, until each one has a thriving, vibrant, indigenously led body of Christ large enough to reach its own people.

To do this we cross barriers of language, suspicion and hostility as well as barriers geographically, culturally, racially, religiously, philosophically, socially and ideologically. Just as Jesus broke through every barrier separating us from God and our inheritance in His Kingdom, we cross (and break down) an infinite number of barriers in order that all men, women and children might experience the restoration meant for them in the Kingdom of God. Only through every believer taking up their responsibility might all peoples have opportunity to turn from darkness to light, embracing the living God, confessing His name, worshipping Him with a thankful heart of love.

Kingdom disciples are being educated, inspired and activated in Jesus' Great Commission. They hear His words in each of the commission passages in the four Gospels. They don't assume this mandate is for somebody else, rightly discerning they are for every born-again believer. Jesus' commission is recorded in each of the four Gospels, Matthew, Mark, Luke and John. It is also included in Acts.

In Matthew 28:18-20, Jesus gives His final instructions before He ascends to the right hand of the Father: "And Jesus came and spoke to them, saying, *"All authority has been given to Me in heaven and on earth. Go therefore and make disciples of all the nations, baptizing them* *in the name of the Father and of the Son and of the Holy Spirit, <u>teaching</u> <u>them to observe all things that I have commanded you</u>; and lo, I am with you always, even to the end of the age."*

In Mark 16:15-18: *"And He said to them, "<u>Go into all the world and preach</u> <u>the gospel to every creature.</u> 16 He who believes and is baptized will be saved; but he who does not believe will be condemned. And these signs will follow those who believe: In My name they will cast out demons; they will speak with new tongues; they will take up serpents; and if they drink anything deadly, it will by no means hurt them; they will lay hands on the sick, and they will recover."*

In Luke 24:46-49: *"Then He said to them, "Thus it is written, and thus it was necessary for the Christ to suffer and to rise from the dead the third day, <u>and that repentance and remission of sins should be preached in His</u> <u>name to all nations, beginning at Jerusalem. And you are witnesses of</u> <u>these things.</u> Behold, I send the Promise of My Father upon you; but tarry in the city of Jerusalem until you are endued with power from on high."*

In John 20:21-23: *"So Jesus said to them again, "Peace to you! <u>As the</u> <u>Father has sent Me, I also send you."</u> And when He had said this, He breathed on them, and said to them, "Receive the Holy Spirit. If you forgive the sins of any, they are forgiven them; if you retain the sins of any, they are retained."*

In Acts 1:8: *"But you shall receive power when the Holy Spirit has come upon you; <u>and you shall be witnesses to Me in Jerusalem, and in all Judea</u> <u>and Samaria, and to the end of the earth."</u>*

K. Taking Up Our Primary Assignment (1 Peter 2:9)

God's sovereign rule will be established over all peoples. God has promised this through Scripture. Where Israel failed to be a *"light to the Gentiles,"* the body of Christ is now called to its primary assignment of abandoned devotion to Jesus and, from the overflow of this love, reaching the world. Where Israel failed to be the set apart *nation* to diffuse the purpose of God, the body of Christ is a *holy nation* (1 Peter 2:9) with the same calling. The body of Christ's mandate flows from Jesus' redemptive victory and His calling out a "Kingdom" people, proclaiming the King and His Kingdom in word and deed. It springs from the Old Testament mandate in Micah 6:8 to *"act justly, love mercy and walk humbly with our God."*

The coming of the Spirit at Pentecost empowered the people of God to embrace their responsibility to bear the faith received among all peoples. They had received this new assignment from Jesus Himself. Yet they were keenly aware they lacked the ability to work out this huge task in their own ability and strength. They saw plainly the inadequacies they each possessed. In each of the five commission passages mentioned above, Jesus includes the factor of the Holy Spirit enabling His people in their task. We were never meant to attempt His work in our own strength (though a large number of Christians certainly try to). The outpouring of the Holy Spirit at Pentecost provided the impetus for a fresh infusion of spiritual power, enabling believers to effectively obey and walk out Jesus' primary assignment for His Church. Through this event, the Church first broke the bounds of Israel, taking the Kingdom message to non-Jewish peoples in a deliberate manner. Their task was to lovingly persuade all ethnic peoples to become disciples of the Kingdom.

Kingdom citizens recognize that as members of the body of Christ, as the Church, we are the channel God has set up to bring about His plans and purposes in the earth. It has nothing to do with us but with God who fills us and has set up His Kingdom in this way. Out of love, we willingly offer ourselves as His servants in whatever capacity He chooses.

L. Identifying Our Great Commission Roles

Believers align with Jesus' big picture vision and purpose – this Gospel of the Kingdom being proclaimed and demonstrated in spiritual power among all people groups of the world (Matthew 24:14). Every believer has been redeemed to participate in the fulfillment of the

Great Commission. Each has a necessary role (or roles) that God has created them to learn, identify and function in. Are we a giver, a goer (message bearer), an intercessor, a mobilizer, an advocate or a welcomer? Typically, believers function in at least one but often two to three roles during their lifetimes. We talk to the Holy Spirit about which role He has assigned to us. We then become a student of that particular role, growing in our understanding of it and how to most effectively operate in it according to God's will. We are dreaming with God about the great possibilities of how He can use us.

M. Spreading Thriving Church Planting Movements (Acts 19:8-10)

Kingdom citizens partner with Jesus to see thriving, spiritually vibrant, culturally relevant church planting movements among all ethnic peoples of the earth. They become true witnesses, wherever they are scattered, because they have experienced the life-transforming power of His death and resurrection (Acts 8:1).

They do this within their own country, across cultures, as well as going beyond their borders to other nations, producing a global harvest of billions thrust into the Kingdom. To accomplish this, multitudes relocate their families and jobs to the spiritually neediest places on earth. Church planting movements (CPMs) are a vital, biblical, strategic model the Lord is restoring to the body of Christ. They provide the greatest means for reaching all peoples.

A church planting movement is a rapid reproduction of culturally relevant, simple churches that reproduce themselves within the culture over and over again. These happen among unreached and unengaged people groups. In other words, they are disciple making movements where obedient disciples make obedient disciples and reproducing churches make reproducing churches. They make Jesus known and transform lives, relationships and communities. CPMs begin with the idea that they are not trying to simply plant one church but hundreds and maybe thousands of churches. If you plan to plant one church, that is all you will get. If you plan and work toward 100 churches, you will move toward this.

Examples of effective church planting movements include in Indonesia, where 1,200 churches were planted in seven years using this method (all in Muslim-dominated areas). In the Horn of Africa seven years ago, there were six known believers among a particular people group. Now, there are 2,500 fellowships with an average of 30 believers in each. Also in Indonesia, a church planting movement was introduced through a training seminary for pastors. They require their students to implement church planting movements while in seminary. The initial group saw 2,500 come to faith, participating in small group fellowships. The seminary expanded to 14 satellite campuses across Indonesia and has seen 256,000 people come to Jesus using these principles.[xlii]

The end result of church planting movements is a church within walking distance of every person within an ethnic people. A minimum goal is for at least 10% of the population of that ethnic people confessing and obeying Jesus. These movements allow for societal transformation by the power of the Gospel while the people coming to faith are immediately reaching out in mission, reproducing simple churches among unreached and unengaged peoples around them. The rapidly reproduced churches are not traditional. They may not even look like churches to an observer. Yet they are committed to the primary marks of a true church (Acts 2:42) without all the cultural and traditional trappings of "church" that hinder peoples· from wanting to participate.

N. A Voice for True Justice (Isaiah 42:1-4)

God is not only concerned about individuals but families, peoples and even nations. He has put social requirements upon His people. It is God's purpose that His people become a "dwelling place" of His powerful presence, that through them He might rule over all aspects of their social web of relationships and connections. He has called His people with the same title Jesus is known as, *"the light of the world,"* so that His Kingdom power might extend to *"the ends of the earth"* (Isaiah 49:6).

God reveals Himself against racism, nationalism, sexism, prejudice, ethnic superiority and any other tendency of human beings to belittle others made in His own image. He is against exploitation, oppression, forced poverty, abuse of power and the neglect of "the stranger." He is a God of justice, desiring His Kingdom community to stand against injustices in the social order. Isaiah declares about Jesus, *"He will bring forth justice for truth"* (Isaiah 42:3). The cries of the oppressed move His heart. We hear both their cries and He Himself provoking His body, as His hands and feet, to serve one another and those experiencing injustices. These characteristics are to mark the people of God.

Kingdom citizens are a voice against injustice in all forms in every arena of society. We serve the broken, abused, desperate and marginalized of society, seeing them restored to dignity, value and honor. God is a loving, just Father. As those who love and obey Him, He gives us power to treat others justly as well. He puts His Spirit of justice within us to contend for just and fair dealings with the poor. As the Gospel of the Kingdom spreads and multiplies among a particular people, the potential for a more just society arises among them due to the nature of justice, equality, value and worth that God and His Kingdom represent.

O. Walking in New Covenant Power (2 Corinthians 3:7-18)

We demonstrate the power of the Gospel through our lives and words, growing in New Covenant power. Paul emphatically declares in 1 Corinthians 2:4: *"And my speech and preaching were not with persuasive words of human wisdom, but in demonstration of the spirit and of power, that your faith should not be in the wisdom of men but in* the power of God." In the intellectual climate of the body of Christ, we have overlooked the vital fact that the Gospel of the Kingdom is meant to be *demonstrated* as much as *proclaimed.* Paul goes on to teach in 2 Corinthians 3:8, *"How will the ministry of the Spirit not be more glorious?"* The movement of the Spirit, including signs and wonders testifying of Jesus' authority over all, is increasing. We want to align with the Spirit, becoming a channel through which He can flow in communities around us. Kingdom citizens release the works of God while hindering the works of evil and spiritual darkness in their geographical areas. We want to consider each of the signs of the Kingdom mentioned in *Phase Three* and begin "practicing" those we sense God might have given to us.

P. Growing in the Gifts of the Holy Spirit (Romans 12:3-8)

Every believer is called to grow in understanding of and operating in the gifts of the Holy Spirit. Paul clarifies this in 1 Corinthians 12:1 when he writes, *"Now concerning spiritual gifts, brethren, I do not want you to be ignorant."* Both in the ancient world and today, there is much ignorance concerning spiritual gifts. The fulfillment of the Great Commission will not happen apart from the body of Christ walking according to the ordained ways of God. He sent the Holy Spirit to empower His body with supernatural gifts for the purpose of reaping the great harvest He has prepared among all people groups. We want to grow in what one leader has called being "supernaturally natural."[xliii] The Holy Spirit's supernatural power is not meant to be "weird," "fanatical" or "strange." He wants to flow in a natural way through human channels submitted to His leadership. Jesus was not flamboyant in His use of the Spirit's supernatural power. Nor do we need to be. Spiritual gifts are used within local churches as every believer has a contribution to make. They are meant to edify and build up each local community of believers.

Every believer has the supernatural capacity to walk in a dimension of the same three areas of supernatural ministry Jesus Himself walked in. This is because we have the same Holy Spirit within us as Jesus possessed. He proclaimed the Kingdom of God with authority, healed the sick, and delivered the oppressed. The youngest in age or the newest born-again believer in Jesus can be used in these ways because the power is not of them but of Him who is in them.

The New Testament includes three primary passages that provide lists of spiritual gifts: 1 Corinthians 12:8-10, 28; Romans 12:6-8; and Ephesians 4:11. These passages should be studied and prayed over, as we ask the Holy Spirit which gifts we might have. Growing in the gifts of the Spirit means practicing the gifts of the Spirit. The gifts need to be demystified. God wants to help us grow in them through trial and error, learning from mistakes and understanding our gifts more and more.

Q. Embracing Suffering and Persecution (John 16:32-33)

Life in the Kingdom in this age also includes challenges, suffering and persecution. The Kingdom of God has come near, opening the door for all peoples to experience restoration of what was intended before the foundations of the world. Because of this, the mission of the Church includes conflict. The Kingdom of God is relentlessly resisted and opposed by peoples and nations not wanting the brought-near Kingdom. They throw off the rightful reign of Jesus as King. They don't want His leadership. They are blinded by the poison of sin and influenced by the "powers and authorities," who hate what God has made available through the Kingdom. They do everything possible to hold people in bondage so that they cannot see the light. We find this theme repeated in the Old Testament, where His lavish provision, gifts and kindness were consistently met with rejection and rebellion, a people seeking their own way, revealing the evil residing in every human heart.

Yet God overcomes evil with good. Through the cross and resurrection, He conquered the powers and authorities. Jesus has defeated sin, death and evil through laying down His own life. However, in this age, between His first and second comings, opposition, suffering and conflict are the norm of true discipleship in His Kingdom. This conflict between kingdoms is inevitable. Neglecting this necessary part of the message results in people seeing God in a wrong overall light. When difficulties arise, they easily blame God, misunderstanding His purposes in and through the challenges. Offense creeps in.

In John 15:19, Jesus gave His "Upper Room Discourse," final words to the 12 disciples before He is arrested later that evening. He plainly tells them, *"If you were of the world, the world would love its own. Yet because you are not of the world, but I chose you out of the world (a citizen of the Kingdom), therefore the world hates you."* We prepare ourselves and others with the fact that the world's systems, values, hopes and purposes are at odds with those of the Kingdom. Jesus continues in John 16:1-4, *"These things I have spoken to you, that you should not be made to stumble. They will put you out of the synagogues; yes, the time is coming that whoever kills you will think that he offers God service. And these things they will do to you because they have not known the Father nor Me. But these things I have told you, that when the time comes, you may remember that I told you of them."*

Hebrews 11, the "heroes of the faith" chapter, describes victories of great men and women of faith. This chapter is in the New Testament to inspire every believer to pursue God in a growing measure of faith, laying hold of victories the Gospel provides. Consider the following passage in Hebrews 11. The first portion cites glorious victories while the second portion reveals equally glorious realities, yet from a very different perspective:

"And what more shall I say? For the time would fail me to tell of Gideon and Barak and Samson and Jephthah, also of David and Samuel and the prophets: who through faith subdued kingdoms, worked righteousness, obtained promises, stopped the mouths of lions, quenched the violence of

fire, escaped the edge of the sword, out of weakness were made strong, became valiant in battle, turned to flight the armies of the aliens. Women received their dead raised to life again.

Others were tortured, not accepting deliverance, that they might obtain a better resurrection. Still others had trial of mockings and scourgings, yes, and of chains and imprisonment. They were stoned, they were sawn in two, were tempted, were slain with the sword. They wandered about in sheepskins and goatskins, being destitute, afflicted, tormented — of whom the world was not worthy. They wandered in deserts and mountains, in dens and caves of the earth" (Hebrews 11: 32–38).

Who is this describing? The same believers who experienced His deliverances were those who experienced persecutions and suffering. How did they endure? By supernatural "grace" released through the power of the Kingdom upon believers experiencing trouble, persecution, pressure and hardship because they are citizens of the Kingdom. In the midst of trouble, the power of God intervenes, enabling us to endure the situation. The message of suffering, and Jesus' power in the midst of it, is needed for the body of Christ to rightly proclaim the Kingdom among all peoples.

Summary of Phase Four

Phase Four of the Gospel of the Kingdom engages every believer with God's big picture purposes. We each have a particular assignment that feeds into the corporate big assignment of His global Church called the *Great Commission.* Many believers overlook Phase Four. They do so to their own detriment as well as that of the purposes of the Kingdom. May the body of Christ arise with such gratitude for all we've been given that we willingly pour out our lives on the alter of love.

8

PHASE FIVE

The Coming Fullness of the Kingdom

We have thus far moved through four glorious phases of the Gospel of the Kingdom. The Kingdom of God has drawn near to us through the life and ministry of Jesus *(Phase One)*, we have entered that Kingdom by His own life *(Phase Two)*, having shared in its privileges and blessings and having received Kingdom inheritance *(Phase Three)*. By these truths, we are made responsible for the Kingdom in the world *(Phase Four)*.[xliv] We do this with hearts ablaze in love for our King, waiting expectantly for His second coming and His ultimate triumph in the world.

History is moving toward a coming transition from this age to the age to come, from the present age of the Kingdom – inaugurated yet hidden, known only by faith – to the age of the full-fledged Kingdom, in visible power and glory. Old Testament prophecy refers more to Jesus' second coming than His first. The coming transition is the focal point of the entire biblical narrative, leading to the transitioning phase to the age to come. In fact, there are around 150 chapters in the Bible referring to the generation of this transition.[xlv] To put this in perspective, the four Gospels, revealing Jesus' life and ministry (His first coming), total 89 chapters. Jesus, Paul, Peter and John all included this transition in their core teaching among the Churches. They had clear understanding of the events to come and wanted all believers to have that same clarity.

Phase Five of the Gospel of the Kingdom – The 'Brought-Near' Kingdom in This Age Will Be Fully Established in the World by a Glorious Transition to the Next Age Through the Physical and Visible Return of Christ

Human beings want to know what the future will be like. What is coming down the road? Understanding the unfolding process of the end of the present age and its transition to the age to come is necessary to remaining faithful as Kingdom citizens. If believers are not aware of God's unfolding plan revealed throughout Scripture, we will buy into the secular interpretation instead of the Spirit's. This teaching is part of the Gospel of the Kingdom, providing clarity on what to expect at the culmination of this age and into the age to come. We have been guilty of leaving out this critical element based on misunderstandings or a misguided sense that it is not important to the overall message.

Keys to Interpreting Biblical Prophecy

There is much confusion about how to interpret biblical prophecy. Biblical prophecy is multi-layered. There are usually three primary elements of any single biblical prophecy. It is on this point that many mistakes of interpretation are made. This holds true of many (if not most) Old and New Testament prophecies, though there are obvious exceptions.

First, biblical prophecy usually relates to a near-future event that took place historically in time and geographically near in space. The prophet is seeing a coming historic event that would happen in the relatively near future when he spoke. For example, Israel was taken captive to Babylon.

Second, that same prophecy simultaneously relates to a yet-unfulfilled event far into the future (usually related to events surrounding the end of this present age and the second coming of Jesus). The near-future event is an example in historic time and space of a type of event that will happen at the end of the age. The historic event is meant to be studied, providing a glimpse and some details into the kind of experience that will happen farther in the future. The realization of the near-future event inspires confidence that God will do what He has said related to the yet-unfulfilled event farther in the future.

Thirdly, all Scripture is for individual and collective building up in God and can be personalized. Bible prophecy can be "spiritualized" to refer to personal promises from God in our individual families, ministries and circumstances. However, we want to be careful in doing this, not overlooking the actual references being highlighted. Because we often are not aware of the near-future events being referenced nor the farther reaching yet future events, we tend to quickly personalize and "spiritualize" the prophecies. We forget they refer primarily to historic situations as well as yet-future specific fulfillments at the end of the age.

A Literal Interpretation

Part of the confusion of interpreting biblical prophecy surrounds whether or not we take the words literally. We will consider in this phase the primary text of Matthew 24. We see this chapter in a literal light. They are literal prophecies, from the mouth of the Son of God Himself, scanning through the centuries, providing detailed expectations of what is to come. They culminate in a literal fulfillment of the Great Commission and a literal second coming of Jesus to establish His 1,000-year (millennium) physical reign on the earth.

We take Jesus' words literally and at face value. We are given no reason in the text itself not to do so. We let Scripture paint the picture of how things will unfold. We don't make the common mistake of reading into Scripture what is not there to support a particular system of end-times theology (eschatology) we might hold. Safe ground is to let Scripture reveal itself, basing conclusions and expectations on this alone. We believe the concepts revealed in *Phase Five* most align with the biblical narrative as well as the eschatology (study of the end times) of the early Church fathers and theologians throughout Church history.

Why Does This Subject Matter?

Grasping details of the future Kingdom produces confidence in the human heart. It is essential for believers to be rooted in the truths of *Phase Five* of the Gospel of the Kingdom. Without this, it is easy for a casual, lukewarm faith to set in. Knowledge of the coming Kingdom inspires believers to live with an eternal perspective. We don't live merely for this life (temporal things) but instead take an eternal outlook on our lives, recognizing we will live for billions of years in eternity. Our lives find ultimate meaning against the backdrop of the coming Kingdom of God. Today has connection with the future Kingdom. How I live today impacts tomorrow.

A. Jesus Has the Last Word (1 Corinthians 15:20-25)

What we see in the world today is not the last word.[xlvi] Jesus, as Son of Man, will come again, in the glory of His Father, bringing all the angels with Him to administrate the affairs of His Kingdom on earth (Matthew 25:31). Upon His second coming, He will immediately overthrow governments and implement His own divine government over the earth (Daniel 2:44; Revelation 11:15). He will gather and celebrate all that is according to His Kingdom (13:43) and destroy what is against His Kingly reign (Matthew 13:30; 13:41). He will set up divine infrastructure across the whole earth that is fully in line with His values, will and Kingdom purposes. Jesus will orchestrate circumstances during that timeframe so that many of the Old Testament prophecies will be clearly seen and experienced.

Believers will rule with Jesus as He implements His divine rule over the whole earth (Revelation 20:4,6). To these ends, we watch

(Matthew 26:41) – taking notice of the biblical signs and trends while observing their impact on culture. We pray for His Kingdom to come and His will to be done on earth just as it is in heaven (Matthew 6:10). We worship and enjoy our coming Bridegroom, with lamps full of oil (Matthew 25:4), guarding from *"love growing cold"* (Matthew 24:12).

B. Jesus' Two Comings (Matthew 24:29-31)

Both the King's comings are distinct, definite and physical. In the first, He came in humility and obscurity, fully divine and fully human, to inaugurate the spiritual Kingdom for all humanity in this present age. In His second coming, He comes in glory and military power, destroying all that opposes holiness on the earth, establishing His visible, physical Kingdom.

Both the King's comings are instrumental in establishing different processes of the Kingdom of God. His first coming provided a way for all to enter the Kingdom, receiving its inheritance and bearing its responsibility by faith through Jesus' redemptive work. His second coming casts out all that hinders His rule and reign throughout the earth, establishing His visible Kingdom on earth with all in submission to His leadership.

As we near the "birthing" of the ultimate Kingdom, there is greater escalation of His glory, power and manifest presence (Matthew 24:14). We contend in faith for the full expression of His light in the earth (Isaiah 60:1-3). Simultaneously, evil and depravity are escalating with opposition and persecution growing toward the King, His Kingdom and Kingdom citizens (Matthew 24:9-12). The present age is characterized by evil, wickedness and all that is hostile to God. All this is overcome by Jesus' second coming, the rightful King of the earth reigning in open, unhidden glory and power.

C. The Full Restoration of the Kingdom

Jesus' second coming produces the full restoration of the Kingdom lost through the first act of rebellion by Adam and Eve. This is the second of two successive developments toward full restoration. We said in *Phase One* that the Old Testament prophets looked to the future, referring consistently to either one or both of these certain developments: (1) The Kingdom coming near in this age through the first coming of Jesus to redeem those who believe; and (2) the Kingdom's complete restoration in power and glory in the age to come, ridding all evil and wickedness, through Jesus' second coming.

The second coming of Christ brings the divine reversal, resulting in original Kingdom conditions in the world before the fall (Garden of Eden-like conditions). We don't go away to heaven when Jesus returns, instead He brings the conditions of heaven to earth (Matthew 6:10; Ephesians 1:10). As citizens of that established Kingdom, we rule and reign with Him as He implements His holy infrastructure on earth. This is based on how we lived during our lives. Our day-to-day lives– choices made to deliberately follow Him, take up our cross, resist the ways of the flesh – will be written in His book (Revelation 20:15). All disciples will be with Him, but not all will be rewarded with roles in that Kingdom.

D. The Processes of Salvation History (Romans 11:11-36)

In Romans 9-11, Paul details the Jews and their rejection of the Gospel. By His initiative with the Jews back in Genesis 12 through Abraham, God was concerned with all the nations (all the ethnic peoples of the earth). He planned Israel to be His channel of blessing for all peoples. They failed, yet God raised up His Messiah, born a Jewish man, to become Lord of humanity. He Himself became the blessing for all peoples that Israel was intended to become. The Jews were set aside due to failure.

Thus the question is asked, "Do the Jews have a future in the restored Kingdom?" Paul answers profoundly in 11:1-12 - God's rejection is not final (11:1). He has great promises for the Jewish people at the end of the age. The number of Old Testament prophecies referring to Israel's ultimate blessing in the Kingdom of God is vast. In the meantime, they have been set aside, not merely as a judgment but according to a larger storyline God is working among all the peoples (11:11-12).

God has planned the Gospel of the Kingdom to influence every Gentile people group (non-Jewish), producing tremendous fruit, before He opens the floodgates to pour out His Spirit on the Jewish people, bringing about a great revival. Paul makes the astounding statement, *"And so all Israel shall be saved"* (Romans 11:26). We know hermeneutically the use of "all" in Scripture does not necessarily mean every one, without exception. We are to understand a large majority of living Jews globally will come to true faith in Yeshua at that time.

In verse 25, Paul states, *"That blindness in part has happened to Israel until the fullness of the gentiles has come in."* Since Old Testament times, blindness among Jews has persisted related to knowing God. It could be said today that Jews are among the most spiritually hardened peoples. Blindness happened with a particular intent in God's heart, lasting only as necessary to accomplish His plan among all people groups globally.

When will their blindness be lifted? When the Great Commission is fulfilled and a large percentage of every non-Jewish ethnic people has become born again, filled with the Spirit, living for the Kingdom of God (Revelation 7:9). This will culminate in the final few years, during the Great Tribulation, when intense pressure is filling the earth. Great trouble will cause hunger for God to rise like at no other time in history. Multitudes will flood into the Kingdom as the Gospel is proclaimed with penetrating clarity, signs and wonders. It is then that the great harvest among every people group will take place, with potentially a billion people coming to saving faith in Jesus in the span of just a few years.

This will provoke Jews, also hearing the message, to great jealousy. This provoking, combined with the pressure Jews will face at the hands of Antichrist, will draw a large number of Jews to Jesus as Messiah. Paul is able to say, *"All Israel (alive at that time) will be saved."* Subsequently, upon Jesus' second coming, Jewish leaders will welcome Jesus into Jerusalem, declaring, *"Blessed is He who comes in the name of the Lord"* (Matthew 23:39). This event will complete the great reversal of Israel's crucifixion of Jesus in His first coming. They will be ushered into His Millennial Kingdom, along with billions of saints from "all peoples," to reign with Jesus on the earth in glory.

E. What Is the Day of the Lord?

The biblical concept of the "Day of the Lord" needs consideration (Isaiah 2:12, 13:6; Jeremiah 46:10; Joel 1:15; 2:11; Obadiah 15; Zephaniah 1:14; Zechariah 14:1; Malachi 4:5; Acts 2:20; 1 Thessalonians 5:2). The Old Testament emphasizes a future season when God directly intervenes in history, a time when this present age gives way to the age to come. The New Testament broadens this central concept.

Through anticipation of the coming "Day of the Lord," we grasp crucial truths: (1) God has not forsaken the world. Though this age is generally an evil one, God is working out His purposes in the earth. (2) Though we see an increase of evil in the earth, we are not to be discouraged. The Old and New Testaments reveal that a breakdown of morality and social order comes before the "Day of the Lord." (3) The heart of God is on display. Though the judgments of Revelation are sure, through His second coming, Jesus will re-create the earth free from all evil influence. He is in full control.

The "Day of the Lord" is a season, not a particular day. Scripture reveals a broad season while also referring to a narrow timeframe. The broad "Day of the Lord" begins at the midpoint of the final seven-year period when the Great Tribulation commences. It runs all the way through (1) the seven seals, trumpets and bowls of wrath; (2) the fulfillment of the Great Commission; (3) the visible, physical second coming of Christ and His entering into Jerusalem; (4) the first resurrection of the saved dead throughout all history at the time of Jesus' return; and (5) the 1,000-year millennium itself. It includes (6) the second resurrection of the unsaved dead and subsequent Great White Throne judgment at the end of the millennium.

There is also a narrow "Day of the Lord," referring to the timeframe of two or so months when Jesus returns in the sky, proceeds around the world, and touches down in Jordan (Isaiah 63:1-6), finally entering Jerusalem. The narrow "Day of the Lord" comes after the cosmic disturbances of the sixth seal mentioned in Joel 2:31 and confirmed in Matthew 24:29. It follows the great falling away of millions who followed Jesus according to their own definitions and the revelation of Antichrist (2 Thessalonians 2:3; 1 Timothy 4:1). It also follows the great harvest as every ethnic people group will have multitudes of thriving, spiritually vibrant local churches within walking distance of every person (Matthew 24:14; Revelation 7:9).

F. Signs and Trends Preceding His Second Coming (Matthew 24:4-14)

The second coming of Christ is preceded by growing signs in the earth. This staggering event does not happen in a vacuum. Matthew 24 provides clear progression of what will precede His second coming.

Verses 4-8 characterize trends throughout the age that are increasing in impact as history progresses. The eight signs Jesus mentions as the _"beginning of birth pains"_ reveal the general state of things between the first and second coming of Jesus: (1) False Christ's deceiving many; (2) hearing of wars and rumors of wars; (3) ethnic hatred, terrorism and genocide; (4) famines; (5) pestilences/

diseases; (6) hearing of earthquakes and their negative effects; (7) commotions; and (8) fearful sights and great signs from heaven.

These eight are present in varying degrees throughout the age, while our hearing of them and feeling a measure of their pain will be increasing toward the end of the age. Each trend has been seen throughout history but will be increasing in intensity as the age progresses and Satan rages against the Church. This culminates with Satan's all-out attempt to obliterate Israel and destroy the Church during the tribulation.

Verses 9-14 are focused on the height of intensity during the "final seven years" prior to Jesus' second coming. They reveal characteristics seen throughout the course of the age but culminating in a level never before seen in history. Characteristics and trends culminating in the "final seven years" in a global, universal manner are: (1) A great increase in persecution covering the earth; (2) social anarchy; (3) false prophets; (4) lawlessness producing the great falling away; and (5) great pressures globally producing the great global harvest.

G. The Abomination of Desolation – the Key Sign (Matthew 24:15)

In Matthew 24:15-22, Jesus provides details of events at the midpoint and second half of the final seven-year period. This is the three-and-a-half year period often referred to as the "Great Tribulation." The challenging events and activities of verses 9-14 will be still taking place. They have not ceased, continuing to escalate. Jesus now reveals the difficulties will come to a head and clarifies the primary sign that transitions into the final three-and-a-half year period. In verse 15, Jesus instructs that the *abomination of desolation* is the key event to understanding the unfolding timeframe.

Though Jesus brought attention to many other signs leading to the end of the age, the *abomination of desolation* is the only political event mentioned, revealing His people are in the immediate three-and-a-half years prior to His second coming. This event is the primary sign to His Church that the Great Tribulation has begun. Jesus points to the book of Daniel to understand the concept of the *"abomination of desolation."*

The *"abomination of desolation"* is mentioned eight times in the Bible. Daniel discussed the concept four times (8:13; 9:27; 11:31; 12:11) and Jesus twice (Matthew 24:15; Mark 13:14). It is also described by Paul (2 Thessalonians 2:3-4) and John (Revelation 13:12-18). We best understand the concept by considering all the instances together. The *"abomination of desolation"* refers to acts of abomination toward God leading to destruction (or desolation) of many peoples and nations.

For an in-depth study on this subject, see the author's study on these concepts entitled *Studies in Matthew 24-25: A Call To Faithfulness In the End Times* (IGNITE Media, 2018)

H. The Great Tribulation (Matthew 24:16-22)

These verses reveal a state of trouble, difficulty and challenge unprecedented in the history of the Church. After Antichrist desecrates the temple in Jerusalem, there comes a time of distress unlike anything previously seen. In Revelation 11:2 and 13:5, it is a specific, three-and-a-half year period of time triggered by the *abomination of desolation*, brought to a merciful end by the literal second coming of Christ. This is a focused, intense three-and-a-half year period, when Satan unleashes his rage upon the Church globally through the Antichrist, the False Prophet and his worshipping hordes.

Many believers will die as martyrs during that period (Revelation 6:9-11). Believers will be unable to buy and sell without the mark of the beast (Revelation 13:17). Jesus will be supernaturally supplying for His people and making ways of escape for many. Yet, it is not merely a story of doom and gloom. Simultaneously, it will be a time when the Church arises like never before (Isaiah 60:1-3), shining the glory of God, brought together in unity as Jesus prayed in John 17, standing in faith, even unto death. This supernatural living will usher in the great harvest and fulfillment of the Great Commission at the end of this three-and-a-half year period.

To remain faithful during that difficult yet glorious timeframe, it is necessary to strengthen muscles of faithfulness now in the midst of pressures. Because the body of Christ will go through this tribulation, required to stand fast in loyalty and faithfulness to Jesus, it is important to grow in doing so in our current situations. When we face challenges, we don't draw back but embrace them, inviting the Spirit to expand our capacity to be steady. This is the testimony of Scripture, how believers prepare for the coming day of trouble if we should be alive to experience it.

I. What About the Church?

A foundational biblical teaching is the Church will never suffer the wrath of God. Some see this meaning the Church must be "raptured" before the Great Tribulation occurs. It is insisted God will not allow His redeemed to experience the Great Tribulation. However, this overlooks Scripture. God did not withhold judgment but released it while Israel was present, yet protected. A primary example is the protection of the Israelites during the 10 plagues from God upon Pharaoh and Egypt. The Israelites were divinely protected in the midst of judgments happening all about them. This view also overlooks that saints experience the rage of Antichrist and Satan, not the wrath of God, through the Revelation judgments.

We find in Scripture only evidence to support the idea that the Church will be on earth throughout the entire period of the Great Tribulation. The release of the seven seals, trumpets and bowls of wrath by the hand of God will be happening, yet the Church is divinely protected from experiencing it, similar to the Israelites in Egypt.

Verses used to advocate that it is impossible for God to allow His children to experience the Great Tribulation include 1 Thessalonians 5:9 and Revelation 3:10. The 1 Thessalonians passage states, _"For God appointed us not unto wrath, but unto the obtaining of salvation through our Lord Jesus Christ."_ Since God hasn't appointed the church to wrath, we must be removed during the time of Tribulation, as He Himself will be pouring out judgment against the Antichrist and his global allies at that time. It is true that God will never allow His people to suffer His wrath. This verse, however, is not speaking about the Tribulation nor the rapture, nor does it teach the removal of the Church from the world but rather a promised deliverance in the midst of trouble. The Revelation passage reveals the same. God does not promise to remove the Church from _"the hour of trial"_ but preserve and deliver her in and through it. This understanding is consistent with the whole counsel of Scripture as to the ways of God in the midst of trouble. He does not remove us from trouble but is present with us in the midst of it, releasing great empowering to overcome.

J. How the Book of Revelation Fits in (Rev 6; Rev 8-9; Rev 16)

It is important to put the different end-time biblical accounts together to understand what is unfolding. The judgments of God revealed in the book of Revelation all take place during these same last three-and-a-half years.

First, the seven seals of Revelation 6 are released by Jesus. It is necessary to grasp the storyline. Jesus Himself is releasing the Antichrist as the first seal to lure wicked humanity's hearts to him. Jesus knows humanity's appetite against Him and is sovereignly allowing Antichrist to deceive multitudes, raising an army against God. Allowing the most demonized man in all history to influence multitudes against God is one of the judgments against wicked humanity. Jesus will later utterly destroy Antichrist and all who stood with him.

The seven seals do not happen all at once but are released one by one over a period during the final three-and-a-half years. We will be able to count them and see them happening in our midst. These include: (1) Antichrist's conquest of political and economic aggression (6: 1-2); (2) military conflict in the form of world war (6: 3-4); (3) economic crisis – famine (6: 5-6); (4) 1/4 of the earth's population dies – sword, hunger, death, beasts (6: 7-8); (5) martyrs crying to God (6:9-11); (6) cosmic and seismic signs creating fear (6:12-17); and (7) release of the seven trumpets (8:1-2).

Next, the seven trumpets of Revelation 8-9 continue one by one over the span of the final three-and-a-half years and include: (1) 1/3 of trees and grass burned up (8:7); (2) 1/3 of seas become blood – 1/3 fish killed and ships destroyed (8:8-9); (3) 1/3 fresh water – rivers and springs – destroyed (8:10-11); (4) 1/3 lights darkened (8:12-13); (5) 1st woe – five months of torment of demonic locusts (9:1-12); (6) 2nd woe – 1/3 of mankind dies – an army of 200 million (9:13-21); and (7) Jesus' second coming process begins (11:15-19).

The 7th Trumpet begins the process of Jesus' second coming (1 Corinthians 15:52; 1 Thessalonians 4:16). The seven bowls of wrath, then, following the seven trumpets culminate during a 30-day period (Daniel 12:11) through Jesus Himself, physically on the earth, bringing destruction to the Antichrist empire on His way to Jerusalem. The Armageddon war is taking place during these final three-and-a-half years, concluding with the seventh bowl of wrath released by Jesus to end the Armageddon war. The seven bowls of wrath take place much faster (30-day period) than the seals and trumpets (over the three-and-a-half years) as they are the final judgments of God released on Antichrist and his global alliances.

The seven bowls of wrath include: (1) Foul and loathsome sores (16:2); (2) sea becomes blood – all fish die (16:3); (3) fresh water becomes blood (16:4-7); (4) sun scorches with heat and fire (16:8-9); (5) darkness and great pain (16:10-11); (6) demonic gathering of kings to Armageddon (16:12-16); and (7) final fall of Babylon – earthquakes and hail (16:17-21).

When considering the detail of these judgments of God, we recall the power and devastation of the 10 plagues against Pharaoh and Egypt in the book of Exodus. Those plagues were a foreshadowing of destruction happening on a global scale during the last three-and-a-half years on the wicked allied with the Antichrist against God.

Let us be reminded that the seals, trumpets and bowls of wrath are not released upon believers on the earth during the last three-and-a-half years. Though believers will be on earth facing the rage of Antichrist and Satan (Revelation 13:7; 17:6), the judgments of God revealed in the book of Revelation are focused entirely upon Antichrist and those siding with and worshipping him. The Church of Jesus Christ will be divinely protected. This protection relates to the seven seals, trumpets and bowls released by Jesus but not necessarily from the tribulation unleashed by Antichrist and Satan during those tumultuous years.

K. What Is the Second-Coming Process?

Above, we concluded the "Day of the Lord" is a season, not one day. The second-coming process is part of that season, itself being a season. Usually, when Jesus' second coming is taught, it is in the context of an instantaneous event. Instead, Scripture relates a different idea. Jesus' second coming includes three distinct processes: (1) His coming in the sky, being seen by every eye (Matthew 24:30; Revelation 1:7). This includes the rapture. (2) Then His "touching down" with His Bride and all the hosts of heaven near modern-day Jordan. He then proceeds to cross land from Jordan to Jerusalem (Isaiah 63:1-6; Revelation 19:11-16; Habakkuk 3:3-18; Psalm 110:5-6). (3) The third process includes His entering Jerusalem to end the Armageddon campaign with a great slaughter. He is then welcomed by Israel's political and spiritual leaders as their King (Matthew 23:39; Psalm 24:7-10; Zechariah 14:4). This three-phase process takes at least 30 days (Daniel 12:12), happening at the same time Jesus is releasing the seven bowls of wrath.

L. The Glorious Appearing of Christ (Matthew 24:29-31)

Matthew 24:29-31 describes the first step of the second-coming process. We are told the *"sign of the Son of Man"* will appear in heaven. Some assume this refers to some specific sign we will see alerting us that He is coming. The text does not suggest this. Instead, the text implies the Son of Man Himself is the sign all things are coming to a head. The unveiling process of His return is the sign the Kingdom of God is coming in all authority, destroying all that opposes God. Christ will descend to earth out of the clouds just as He ascended in Acts 1:11. There is no comparison in human history to this event. We try to conjure up in our imaginations what it might be like and simply can't. This will be a public event, with every eye of every living person on the planet seeing Him. Yet, it does not happen instantaneously. For every eye to see Him would mean His coming takes at least a full day. How else would every person around the world be able to physically see Him with their own eyes?

M. The Accompanying Rapture (Matthew 24:31)

The second coming of Christ is the seventh trumpet in Revelation 11:15-18. We are told in Matthew 24:31 that Jesus will send His angels *"with the sound of a trumpet, and they will gather together His elect from the four winds, from one end of heaven to the other."* This event is the *"catching up"* in the air of all believers who have previously physically died. They are resurrected and, along with all believers still alive on the earth, are given spiritual bodies and "caught up" with Christ. This is what Paul saw in 1 Thessalonians 4:15-17 and 1 Thessalonians 3:13. This uncountable group will together accompany Christ to the earth. They don't all go away to heaven as is usually understood. The word used in the New Testament related to Jesus' second coming is *"parousia."* This word can best be translated as either "coming," "arrival" or "presence." The *"parousia"* includes the rapture of the Church, the raising of the righteous dead, and the destroying of

Antichrist (2 Thessalonians 2:8).

It is at this time that believers are rewarded by Jesus for how they lived in this age. In 1 Corinthians 3:13, Paul helps us understand that *"each ones' work will become clear, for the Day will declare it, because it will be revealed by fire; and the fire will test each one's work, of what sort it is."* The word "work" is best understood as our actions, behaviors, motives, decisions, and values and how we aligned our lives overall with His own. Some believers' "work" will be like wood, hay and straw, done with the wrong motive and intent, while others will be like gold, silver and precious stones for the glory and pleasure of God, not self or man. Eternal rewards will be applied in the Millennial Kingdom through certain assignments from the Lord and on into the eternal state.

Most scholars and Bible expositors agree the second coming of Christ takes place at the end of the Tribulation. However, there is debate about when the "rapture" takes place. The most common, popularized teaching today is that Jesus returns just for His church, gathering her out from the world, before the Tribulation. Thus, there are two comings of Jesus - one in secret for His church at the beginning of the Tribulation and one in glory for all to see at the end of the Tribulation.

Though a popular teaching, we do not find biblical evidence supporting this viewpoint, only evidence of one coming of Jesus, which includes the gathering of all the saints at the end of the Tribulation. This includes both believers alive at the time and the resurrection of all the saved who died throughout history. Many believers have ignored the Great Tribulation, having been taught it doesn't apply to the Church, as all believers will have been removed by the Lord by this time. We believe this is an incorrect teaching producing much harm in the body of Christ.

N. Defeating His Spiritual Enemies (Colossians 2:15)

What is the purpose behind the second coming of Christ? A crucial part of Jesus' mission in His first coming was overthrowing the power of Satan (1 John 3:8). Paul states this took place through the death and resurrection of Jesus: *"He disarmed the principalities and powers and made a public spectacle of them, triumphing over them in Him"* (Colossians 2:15). A consistent teaching of the New Testament is that, through resurrection from the dead and ascension to the right hand of the Father, Jesus won victory over the powers of darkness. Jesus' ministry of delivering people from demonic bondage was evidence the Kingdom of God had broken into history, inaugurated by His first coming. Through resurrection and ascension, Jesus was enthroned beside the Father in power and authority, ruling and reigning as King. Throughout history and today, people continue to be delivered from darkness and spiritual bondage, transferred into the Kingdom of God. Yet, this is done in a hidden way. The world is not aware of such events as things continue on the surface as though Jesus had never come.

Though Satan has been defeated and human beings are now free to choose God in their lives, he still wields tremendous power across the earth. As a result, the nations ignore God and His Kingdom. This will not continue forever. Satan's final defeat at the hands of Jesus will take place in two successive stages still in the future. First, at the beginning of the millennium, he will be bound and chained, unable to deceive the nations throughout the 1,000-year time period (Revelation 20:1). At the end of the millennium, Jesus will release him from this captivity and Satan will again be free to deceive (Revelation 20:7). He will do this for a very short time, finding people's hearts still prone to deception, and then mass an army to defeat the reigning King again. God will cast him down a final time, throwing him into the lake of fire, never again to have any evil influence (Revelation 20:10).

This situation is one reason why the second coming of Christ is necessary. He is coming to complete and enforce the work begun through His first coming. All enemies of God will be put under Jesus' feet (1 Corinthians 15:25); all will be subject to His rule and reign. At His second coming, He will manifest the power and glory hidden in His first coming for all to see in outward splendor.

From the time of Jesus' second coming through the Millennium and on into the eternal state itself, the Kingdom of God will be experienced in open glory. The hidden nature of the Kingdom is a characteristic of the present age, while the second coming reveals a visible, triumphant, victorious Kingdom of God. Never will the Kingdom revert back to the hidden state we currently experience. The second coming provides absolute victory for the Church, forever experiencing the fullness of God. This glorious future is assured by Jesus.

O. Bringing Complete Salvation to His Saints

Another reason Jesus is coming again is to complete the salvation of believers. There are three tenses of salvation used in the New Testament. We have *been* saved, *are being* saved and *will be* saved. This can be broken down in theological terms as our justification, sanctification and glorification. As born-again believers on this earth, we are in process. There was a definite moment when we believed Jesus has forgiven our sins, experienced the new birth, and entered the Kingdom of God. We took His leadership in our lives, submitting to Him and His purposes. We had assurance of salvation and were justified, "saved."

Next, the process of ongoing sanctification continues throughout our lifetimes. The Holy Spirit is continually refining us, delivering us, purifying us. We are continually pressing onward and upward in becoming more like Jesus in every way. If embracing this process, we are being continually "saved." Sanctification reaches its pinnacle when we are restored to our original condition before the fall at the second coming of Christ. This ultimate "salvation" will happen when we are raised with Christ, receiving spiritual, resurrected bodies like Jesus' own (1 John 3:2). This is the promise of Matthew 24:31 – when Christ gathers all believers to Himself, bringing us to the earth to reign together with Him in His ultimate Kingdom forever (Revelation 20:4-6).

P. To Reign Over the Whole Earth (Revelation 11:15)

Jesus is coming back to earth to physically rule over kings and governments for an extended period of time. The book of Revelation helps us understand this. In Revelation 11:15, the angels in heaven sing and shout, rejoicing over a massive change in governments on the earth. *"The kingdoms of the world have become the Kingdoms of our Lord and of His Christ and He shall reign forever and ever."* This event happens as part of the process of the second coming of Christ. It is an unwanted, hostile takeover by Jesus of all the governments of the earth, achieved through a great battle, producing horrific bloodshed. Jesus is returning as a warrior King, taking vengeance on all standing defiantly against His rule.

Q. The Millennial Kingdom (Rev 20:1-10)

As we have seen, there are two primary divisions of time in the Old Testament referred to as "this present age" and the "age to come," with the second coming of Jesus as the dividing marker. Jesus, in the Gospels, generally taught the end of the age through the lens of this Jewish mindset. His parables of the Kingdom in Matthew 13 related to this division of time. The New Testament includes much of this same language.

The book of Revelation, however, broadens this central understanding of time, specifically through Revelation 20, where an additional period of 1,000 years is revealed to John. This adds a new dimension to the Old Testament understanding of time needing to be understood. The age to come, through Revelation 20, is understood as including: (1) the 1,000-year reign of Jesus on earth following His second coming – v. 4; (2) the release of Satan to deceive people once more and his ultimate banishment to hell by God – v. 7; (3) the second resurrection and judgment of the unsaved dead before the Great White Throne – vs. 11-13; (4) the making of the new heavens and new earth – 21:1; and (5) the eternal state in the New Jerusalem – 21:10.

Revelation 20:1-9 reveals the 1,000-year reign of Jesus over all kingdoms, mentioned in Revelation 11:15. The millennium follows His second coming yet is before the final judgment and the creation of the new heaven and new earth. This passage also specifies its length – 1,000 years – and is repeated six times in this passage. The millennium is the period of time when Jesus restores all things on earth as they were before the fall of humanity in Genesis 3. The 1,000-year period will be a great manifestation of the Kingdom of God as intended in the heart of God before the foundation of the world. Jesus will gradually refine every infrastructure throughout the earth according to His divine will and plans from His headquarters in Jerusalem.

It is during this timeframe that the event highlighted in Ephesians 1:10 is taking place. Paul reveals *"that in the dispensation of the fullness of times He might gather together in one all things that are in heaven and on earth – in Him."* Usually, this verse is described as the bringing together of the saints, both in heaven and alive on the earth, at the time of His return. This is undoubtedly part of this picture, but it is much bigger than this. The power, wisdom, creativity, love, purity, righteousness and justice marking the heavenly realm right now will come down to the earth, becoming one entity. No longer will the earthly and heavenly realms be separated. They will comingle. It is this comingling that creates the ultimate environment of heaven on earth, the Kingdom of God in complete operation on earth. This is what Abraham saw when he longed for a city that has foundations, whose builder and maker is God (Hebrews 11:10). Many interpret the "city" Abraham sees as heaven. More likely, it is the New Jerusalem (a physical city) descending and connecting with the earthly Jerusalem as the center of operations from which Jesus rules and reigns in the Millennial Kingdom.

R. Millennial Kingdom Glimpses in Scripture

The Old Testament prophets saw glimpses of what the millennium would be like. Many chapters in the Bible refer to this timeframe. We do ourselves disservice in understanding the Bible when we spiritualize these chapters and verses, making of them something never intended. We often are looking for these happenings in this age when Scripture refers to their appearance in the Millennial Kingdom.

Some of these glimpses include *"the earth will be filled with the knowledge of the Lord, as the waters cover the sea"* (Isaiah 11:9; Habakkuk 2:14); *"every knee will bow and every tongue confess that Jesus Christ is Lord to the glory of God the Father"* (Isaiah 45:23; Philippians 2:10-11); *"the Lord will be King over the whole earth"* (Zechariah 14:9); and *"they shall beat their swords into ploughshares and their spears into pruning hooks"* (Isaiah 2:4; Micah 4:3). These events will not happen until the Millennial Kingdom.

Other scriptural images of that timeframe include Isaiah 65:20 revealing that death at 100 years of age will be a tragic premature loss; nature itself will be revolutionized under the physical reign of King Jesus, *"the wolf will live with the lamb..."* (Isaiah 11:6-7); carnivores will become herbivores as God intended (Genesis 1:30); and children will play safely among animals that are wild in this age but will be calm in the age to come (Isaiah 11:8). This is the time when believers, both Jew and Gentile alike, will *"reign on the earth with Christ"* (Revelation 5:10) as well as the time when believers *"from every tribe, language, tongue, people and nation"* will be appointed to lead governments under Jesus' authority (Revelation 5:9; Luke 19:15-19; 1 Corinthians 6:2; 2 Timothy 2:12) and when the *"meek will inherit the earth"* (Matthew 5:5).

Summary of Phase Five

Phase Five of the Gospel of the Kingdom enables believers to take an eternal perspective, living for that which really matters. We grasp the processes Scripture reveals of how history will unfold. We marvel at the ways of God in restoring the Kingdom and the glorious wisdom and processes He uses to do so. Together, all Five of these Phases are used of God to draw millions into His Kingdom, grow them in spiritual maturity through embracing His full inheritance while proving responsible for what He has entrusted to the church, prepared for what is to come and living for eternity with hearts burning for our great King. *"Come Lord Jesus! Take Your Throne! Let Your Kingdom Come and Your Will Be Done Here on Earth As It Is In Heaven!"*

NOTES

i.   Arthur F Glasser, *Announcing the Kingdom: The Story of God's Mission in the Bible* (Grand Rapids, MI, Baker Academic, 2003) p.7

ii.   Ibid, p. 8

iii.   G. Campbell Morgan, *The Teaching of Christ* (London, UK, Pickering and Inglis LTD, 1946) p.174

iv.   Ibid, p. 164

v.   George Eldon Ladd, *The Gospel of the Kingdom: Scriptural Studies in the Kingdom of God* (Grand Rapids, MI, Eerdmans Publishing Company, 1959) p. 24

vi.   Ibid, p. 24

vii. Ibid, p. 31

viii. Morgan, *The Teaching of Christ*, p. 164

ix.   David and Paul Watson, *Contagious Disciple-Making: Leading Others on a Journey of Discovery* (Thomas Nelson, 2014) p. 27

x.   Roland Allen, *Spontaneous Expansion of the Church* (Eugene, OR, Wipf and Stock Publishers, 1997) p. 52

xi.   Glasser, *Announcing the Kingdom*, p.263

xii. Definition from www.JoshuaProject.com under definition of unreached people groups

xiii. Morgan, *The Teaching of Christ*, p.171-172. Morgan highlights five phases, which have been adapted, as the crucial elements of Jesus' teaching on the Kingdom of God

xiv.   Donald McGavran, *Understanding Church Growth* (Grand Rapids, MI, Eerdman's Publishing Company, 1990) p. 123

xv.   Ibid, p.116

xvi.   Definition of "Worldview" from Collins English Dictionary Online

xvii.   Watson, *Contagious Disciple-Making*, p. 24

xviii. Watson, *Contagious Disciple-Making*, p. 13

xix.   Paul E Pierson, Themes from Acts (Ventura, CA, Regal Books, 1982) p. 115

xx.   Allen, *Spontaneous Expansion of the Church*, p. 55

xxi.   Glasser, *Announcing the Kingdom*, p. 32

xxii.   Ibid, p. 31

xxiii. Ibid, p. 35

xxiv.   Ibid, p. 38

xxv.   Mike Bickle, *Study Notes on the Beauty of God in Creation* – www.mikebickle.org

xxvi.   Ibid

xxvii. Eric Metaxas, *Martin Luther: The Man Who Rediscovered God and Changed the World* (New York, New York, Viking Books, 2017) p. 97

xxviii. Glasser, *Announcing the Kingdom*, pgs. 202-210

xxix.   Pierson, *Themes from Acts*, p. 20

xxx.   Pierson, *Themes from Acts*, p. 9

xxxi.   Morgan, The Teaching of Christ, p.170

xxxii. Ibid, p.172

xxxiii. Ladd, *The Gospel of the Kingdom*, p. 97

xxxiv. Ibid, p. 98

xxxv.   Ladd's chapter in The Gospel of the Kingdom on *"The*

Demand of the Kingdom" is a crucial chapter providing a powerful overview of the concepts in this portion of Phase Two.

xxxvi.   Mike Bickle, Study Notes, *The Revelation of the Free Gift of God's Righteousness*, September 28, 2012

xxxvii.   Dean S. Gilliland, *Pauline Theology and Mission Practice* (Eugene, OR, Wipf and Stock Publishers, 1998) p. 146

xxxviii.   Ibid, p. 154

xxxix.   C. Peter Wagner, *Acts of the Holy Spirit: A Modern Commentary on the Book of Acts* (Ventura, CA, Regal Books, 2000) p. 112

xl.   Wagner, *Acts of the Holy Spirit*, p. 93

xli.   Pierson, *Themes From Acts*, p. 21

xlii.   Stories shared at Ethne 2012 Conference in Seoul, Korea

xliii.   This is a phrase coined by John Wimber, the founder of the Vineyard Church movement, in the 1980's

xliv.   Morgan, *The Teaching of Christ*, p. 175

xlv.   Mike Bickle, *Study Notes*, 150 Chapters on the End Times, October 3, 2008

xlvi.   Morgan, *The Teaching of Christ*, p. 179

**GLOBAL
MISSION
MOBILIZATION
INITIATIVE**

*" The Lausanne Committee for World Evangelization enthusiastically affirms the work and vision of GMMI. GMMI's commitment to mobilizing & equipping the global church toward its role in the task of reaching the world
for Christ is compelling and strategic. "*

GlobalMMI.net / info@GlobalMMI.net

>>> **Who We Are:** We are a growing global mission mobilization initiative multiplying national mission mobilization movements mobilizing and equipping local ministries and disciples at every level of the body of Christ.

>>> **What We Do:** We multiply local ministries and disciples for the Great Commission in three primary ways:
1. An international step by step strategy multiplying mission mobilization movements at every ministry level across a national church.
2. A Great Commission Equipping Center (GCEC) in Chiang Mai, Thailand
3. A publishing arm, IGNITE Media, producing high quality mission mobilization and equipping materials and resources.

>>> **Core Objectives:**
1. Movements of individual disciples mobilized and equipped for Jesus' Great Commission
2. Movements of individual local ministries mobilized and equipped for Jesus' Great Commission.

3. Movements of individual denominations and church organizations mobilized and equipped for Jesus' Great Commission.
4. Movements of national evangelical alliances and associations in every nation mobilized and equipped for Jesus' Great Commission,

OTHER RESOURCES FROM IGNITE MEDIA

Cultivating Abandoned Devotion To Jesus

God is calling His people into deeper relationship with Himself. This is the beginning of all effective ministry and the only way effective ministry is continuously sustained. We cultivate this wholeheartedness through studying His Word deeply while applying all we are learning. These Bible studies go deep into heart of God's Word, revealing depths and insight that will revolutionize your spiritual life. These can be used individually or in a group setting.

- Studies in the Life of Joseph
- Studies in the Book of Jonah
- Studies in the Book of Colossians
- Studies in the Sermon on the Mount
- Studies in Jesus' Parables of the Kingdom (Matthew)
- Studies in the Seven Churches of Revelation
- Studies in Matthew 24 - 25 Jesus' End-Times Discourse

Mobilizing Local Ministries

The Holy Spirit is raising a vision of not merely one by one mission mobilization, but the concept of mobilizing and equipping whole local ministries for Jesus' Great Commission.

These resources enable that process through the use of proven tools and teaching. Each of these resources serve a unique purpose toward seeing disciples mobilized and equipped through local ministries to serve the unreached.

- Handbook for Great Commission Ministries (English, Spanish, French, Chinese (both simplified and traditional), Thai)
- Great Commission Bible Studies
- Global Prayer Teams
- Six Roles in the Great Commission
- Developing a Sending Strategy
- Waking the Giant
- Where's Your Haystack DVD

Equipping For Global Harvest

To see the literal fulfillment of the Great Commission we need to be equipped in particular areas often not discussed or emphasized. These resources provide focus on core areas of equipping the Holy Spirit is emphasizing and that need to be carefully grasped and integrated into our lives if we will be effective.

- Engaging the Holy Spirit
- Declare His Glory Among the Nations
- Proclaiming the Kingdom
- Spiritual Equipping For Mission
- Deeper